CO-TEACH!

Building and Sustaining Effective Classroom
Partnerships in Inclusive Schools

second edition

Marilyn Friend, Ph.D.

2nd edition

Friend, Marilyn

Co-Teach! Building and Sustaining Effective Classroom Partnerships in Inclusive Schools

ISBN 978-0-9778503-1-0

Dedication

To all the co-teachers who do their best to help every one of their students succeed, whether they learn easily or with difficulty, whether they have a privileged life or live in poverty, whether they come to school speaking English or are just learning it, whether they are obedient or disruptive, and whether they indicate they appreciate your efforts or not. You persevere in the face of a challenging economy, criticism in the popular media, and legislative attempts to direct how you do your job. You encourage and support and cajole and insist, and our world is a better place because of your efforts and all the lives you touch. Thank-you for all that you do.

About the Author

 Marilyn Friend, Ph.D., has spent her career as a general education teacher, special education teacher, researcher, professor, administrator, teacher educator, consultant, and staff developer. She is Professor Emerita of Education in the Department of Specialized Education Services at The University of North Carolina at Greensboro, and she is Past President of the Council for Exceptional Children (CEC), the largest international professional organization dedicated to improving the educational success of children and youth with disabilities and/or gifts and talents. Currently, she works with local, regional, and state education agencies to evaluate their special education programs, re-design their special education systems to improve outcomes for students, teach teachers and administrators about co-teaching and inclusion, and problem solve about the implementation of contemporary special education practices.

Dr. Friend's expertise is highly respected nationally and internationally, as evidenced by the more than 3000 presentations and projects she has completed in the United States, Canada, Europe, the Middle East, and Asia. In addition to this handbook, she is the author or co-author of three widely used college textbooks on special education, inclusion, and collaboration; more than 50 articles about collaboration and co-teaching; and the highly popular video series *Power of Two*, featuring real-life examples for teachers and administrators of taking co-teaching and other inclusive practices from concept to reality.

Other Books and Materials by Marilyn Friend

From the Forum on Education
Available at www.forumoneducation.org

The *Power of Two* series, produced by Dr. Leonard Burrello and directed by Mr. Jotham Burrello of Elephant Rock Productions, includes four videos that explain and demonstrate how to create, build, sustain, and evaluate co-teaching as part of inclusive education.   Narrated by Marilyn Friend, these are the video titles with a brief explanation and intended audience for each:

🧩 *Power of Two: Including Students through Co-Teaching* (2nd edition) (2004)

This 1 hour 10 minute video program, divided into five parts so it can be shown as part of brief staff development sessions, outlines all the key components of effective co-teaching programs, illustrating them with footage from actual classrooms at the elementary, middle, and high school levels and punctuated with teacher and administrator interviews.

🧩 **More Power: Instruction in Co-Taught Classrooms** (2010)

This video, for those already familiar with co-teaching basics, presents seven key dimensions of effective instructional practices across K-12 settings: assessment and planning; content, materials, and instruction; the instructional environment; the presentation of instruction; student participation; the evaluation of student performance; and adult interactions. Filmed in classrooms K-12, the video demonstrates how evidence-based practices can be incorporated into co-taught lessons. A brief review of the six co-teaching approaches is included as well.

🧩 **Instructional Power: Co-Teachers Share Instructional Techniques** (2010)

Professionals are always looking for ideas to enhance instruction in their co-taught classes. This video includes a collection of simple yet effective strategies to improve K-12 student engagement and participation. You can use these ideas in both co-taught and solo-taught classes.

Releasing the Power! District and School-Based Leaders on Inclusive Schooling and Co-Teaching (2010)

In this video, district leaders, principals, and other site leaders share how the Charlotte-Mecklenburg Schools went about a very deliberate process for building inclusive practices and implementing co-teaching as part of that philosophical shift. Today CMS is considered a model of what can happen when a district decides to truly address the needs of all students. Visitors from across the country come to CMS to explore how to create similar success. This video can start you on that journey.

From Pearson Publishing

Available at www.pearsonhighered.com (search by author) or www.amazon.com

Including Students with Special Needs: A Practical Guide for Classroom Teachers (6th edition) (Merrill, 2012)

Written with Dr. William Bursuck, this book is the one that more colleges and universities throughout the world use than any other to teach general educators how to meet the needs of students with disabilities or other special needs in their classrooms. It is focused on the practical, filled with case studies and vignettes, and designed to provide educators across grade levels with the most current information to guide their practices, with or without co-teaching.

Interactions: Collaboration Skills for School Professionals (7th edition) (Allyn & Bacon, 2013)

This book is considered the bible of collaboration for school professionals. It is the most widely used book to teach these skills, and it is valuable for teacher candidates, veteran teachers, related services personnel, and administrators. Each concept is illustrated with detailed examples, and the situations outlined are those common for today's educators.

✳ **Special Education: Contemporary Perspectives for School Professionals** (4th edition) (Merrill, 2014)

This book is an overview of the field of special education, but it is much more than that. By presenting case studies at the beginning of each chapter as well as incorporating interviews with parents of children with disabilities, individuals with disabilities, and professionals who work with individuals with disabilities, readers learn about the conceptual and procedural requirements of the field but also about the real stories of real people, including the joys as well as the challenges of their lives.

Coming Soon!
Will be available at www.coteach.com

✳ **Co-Teaching for Administrators: Creating and Sustaining Programs that Improve Outcomes for Students with Special Needs**

Dr. Friend has assisted thousands of school administrators to build co-teaching programs, prepare staff members to implement them, evaluate program effectiveness, address problems and issues that may arise, and create sustainability. This is the book written just for district and site administrators. It emphasizes realistic ideas for resolving the very real challenges that occur in implementing innovative programming to improve student outcomes.
Available: August 2013

✳ **Co-Teaching and Effective Instruction: Maximizing Student Outcomes by Intensifying Teaching and Learning**

After co-teaching is understood as a service delivery option, after professionals form strong partnerships, and after logistics have been addressed, there is still more to achieving the greatest impact from co-teaching. What constitutes effective instruction in a co-taught class? How should IEP or ILP goals be embedded into the general curriculum? That is the focus for this book, intended to complement the other books in this series by focusing on the most essential part of improving student outcomes K-12 -— that is, evidence-based strategies particularly suited to the co-taught classroom.
Available: December 2013

Table of Contents

Preface

Over the past few years, the number of publications on co-teaching has exploded. Journal articles describe specific programs and summarize research on co-teaching effectiveness, blog entries describe both the highs and the lows of co-teaching practice, and books to guide co-teachers and their administrators abound. The first edition of *Co-Teach! A Handbook for Creating and Sustaining Effective Classroom Partnerships in Inclusive Schools* was the first teacher-friendly book on the market, and it remains unique in its depth of information combined with reader friendliness. Here are some of the key updates for this second edition:

- A whole new chapter has been added emphasizing the importance of providing specially designed instruction for students with disabilities and other special needs through co-teaching.

- Information co-teaching as part of programs for English language learners has been significantly increased.

- An updated approach to thinking about, scheduling, and using shared planning time is highlighted.

- Co-teaching is explored as a means of facilitating student learning when implementing the Common Core State Standards (CCSS).

- The latest research, websites, and other resources on co-teaching are included.

- Appended worksheets, activities, and checklists have been updated.

This second edition is the result of my continuing work in schools, districts, and agencies across the country and around the world. It reflects my nearly 40 years of experience teaching children; instructing university students at the undergraduate and graduate levels; staying abreast of the most current trends and issues in the field; and working with teachers and other school professionals, listening to the successes they describe, the challenges they encounter, and the questions they ask. I sincerely hope that you find this handbook has the information about co-teaching that you've been seeking.

Chapters 1 and 2 overview key concepts and the rationale for co-teaching. I am firmly convinced that co-teaching is far more successful if educators understand what it is and what it isn't and the reason why it continues to grow rapidly as a service delivery option for students with disabilities, English language learners, and other pupils with special needs. Chapter 3 focuses on the elements of a strong professional relationship that is the foundation for exemplary co-teaching practice, examining both the interpersonal relationship between teachers and the practical classroom matters they may need to negotiate. Chapter 4 outlines the six co-teaching approaches, variations of them, and factors to consider in selecting them. This chapter also includes examples of co-taught lessons.

Chapter 5 adds a detailed discussion of instruction and how it should be more intense and focused than instruction in a solo-taught class. The goal is not to provide a laundry list of teaching strategies, but instead for educators to understand the type of instruction that must occur as part of co-teaching. Chapter 6 provides specific suggestions for overcoming the most common co-teaching challenge – common planning time, and it also briefly addresses other logistics. Chapter 7 discusses variations in co-teaching practice and applications that extend beyond special education and ESL services, surveying various professionals who may co-teach, unique scheduling options, and co-teaching applications in non-traditional programs and services. Finally, Chapter 8 comprises all the other questions that arise when developing, refining, or sustaining a co-teaching program. Challenges such as the ones included in this chapter may not be able to be avoided, but professionals can prepare to address them and thus better educate students.

I wish you all success in your co-teaching. I look forward to hearing about your accomplishments and to seeing the data that document the positive outcomes you've made in the lives of students with disabilities or other special needs. If you'd like to provide feedback about the book, share your story, or ask a question, contact me at marilynfriend@coteach.com. I can't promise a personal response to everyone, but I'll do my best.

Acknowledgements

One of the questions I'm frequently asked is this: How in the world do you accomplish all that you do -- speaking to groups in the U.S. and other countries, observing in classrooms, consulting with local and state/regional agencies, serving your professional association, guiding graduate students, and writing articles and books? The answer is simple: It is because Bruce Brandon, my husband, soul mate, and chief cheerleader, makes it possible. The support he provides is extraordinary, everything from listening to me work out a problem with my writing, to editing and proofreading chapters, to offering opinions on book design, to cooking meals, to manning what we call "Crisis Central" (computer and phone) on bad travel days. He has said again and again, "I'll help you – any way I can." He means it, and he does it. How fortunate I am to have such a caring spouse.

Right after Bruce, I owe a huge debt of thanks to Sonia Martin, administrative secretary for the Department of Specialized Education Services at the University of North Carolina at Greensboro. She makes time on weekends and holidays to assist me with this project. She edits and proofreads, formats and re-formats, works out design details, and otherwise manages a million bits of minutiae that have to be addressed before a book is published. Her amazing technical skills, diligence, and ability to see humor in even the toughest challenges of producing a book are invaluable. Her answer to any dilemma is, "It'll be alright. I'll just figure it out." And she always does. I'm privileged to know and work with her.

Finally, thanks are offered to all of the professionals across the country who have become colleagues and friends as we have worked together, laughed and sometimes cried together, and tried mightily to improve outcomes for students through inclusive practices and co-teaching. You know who you are, and I wouldn't want to inadvertently embarrass any of you by naming names. It is your stories, dilemmas and solutions to them, and optimism that demonstrate the potential of co-teaching, and every idea and good example in this handbook came from you or the professionals in your schools. I hope you find this compendium of concepts and practices helpful and grounded in the reality of the world of school professionals.

Chapter 1
Key Concepts for Understanding Co-Teaching

Alone we can do so little; together we can do so much.
~ Helen Keller

Learner Objectives

1. Describe what co-teaching is and is not.

2. Explain how co-teaching is related to other educational terms and practices — collaboration, inclusion, and team teaching.

3. Examine the range of contemporary applications of co-teaching.

4. Distinguish between co-teaching and the supports that paraprofessionals may provide.

As a school professional, you have complex and demanding responsibilities. Whether you are a general or special education teacher, an English as a second language (ESL) educator, a speech-language therapist, a reading or math specialist or coach, another special service provider, or an administrator, you are expected to ensure that nearly all students reach today's rigorous academic standards. Your task is complicated by students' increasingly diverse needs. You are charged with challenging those who are gifted and talented, improving the achievement of struggling pupils, and addressing the individualized goals of learners who have disabilities or other special needs while simultaneously reaching those students who do not command extraordinary attention. And you are doing all of this at a time when educators often are criticized in the popular press and when some parents and community members are asking you to do more and more, often with fewer and fewer resources.

Faced alone, the challenges of being a twenty-first century educator can, at times, seem insurmountable. Working collaboratively with colleagues, though, presents opportunities for success that otherwise would not be possible. And that is the basis for this book. Co-teaching — a professional instructional partnership — enables educators to more readily determine students' strengths and weaknesses, to deliver instruction and assess learning more efficiently, and to tailor activities to the exceptional needs that some students have. At the same time, co-teaching provides professionals with a sense of support, that is, the knowledge they can blend their expertise and share the responsibilities of educating their pupils.

Are you thinking of co-teaching in the near future? Already co-teaching and refining your practice? Responsible for creating and evaluating a co-teaching program in a school or district? Just as professionals implementing a new remedial reading program or science curriculum receive professional development so that they implement the program the way it was intended, so, too, do those working with co-teaching need a specific set of knowledge and skills. This is particularly true since many teachers and other educators learned little in their own professional preparation about working in a general education classroom with a colleague. The goal of this book is to provide that knowledge and those skills. The information included is based on the rapidly accumulating professional literature on this topic (for example, Friend, Cook, Hurley-Chamberlain, & Shamberger, 2010; Honigsfeld & Dove, 2012; Isherwood, Barger-Anderson, Merhaut, Badgett, & Katsafanas, 2011; Pearl, Dieker, & Kirkpatrick, 2012; Walsh, 2012), but it also is based on my own work over the past 30 years assisting educators to implement co-teaching in elementary, middle, and high schools in urban, suburban, and rural districts in the U.S. as well as in several other countries. This book is the result of innumerable conversations with teachers and administrators — some enthusiastic and some discouraged — about the power of co-teaching and the problems that sometimes occur in implementing it. It is informed by thousands of observations in classrooms where professionals are closely working together or struggling to find appropriate roles. And it is based on my own firm belief that although no single instructional model is a panacea, co-teaching can significantly and positively enable many educators to reach their most cherished goal, that is, helping their students to truly reach their potential.

What Co-Teaching Is

Successful co-teaching begins with understanding what it is. Here are the essential elements that make co-teaching a unique instructional arrangement.

Co-Teaching is a Service Delivery Option

Depending on needs, students access a wide range of special services in addition to core instruction. Many options exist for offering those services. Some learners are supported when a specialist consults with a general education teacher, as might happen when a psychologist offers suggestions to a teacher for responding to disruptive behavior. Other students leave the classroom to receive specialized instruction, as is the case when those who are English language learners (ELLs) go to a separate classroom for language instruction or those with speech or language needs receive therapy in a small group. Yet other students spend most if not all of their instructional day in a special class setting, usually those with significant disabilities for whom a carefully structured environment with highly specialized supports is necessary.

Co-teaching is similar to these options in that it is a way students receive their services. However, it is also unique. First, the other service models tend to be based on an assumption that the more intense a learner's needs, the more time she or he should spend in a separate setting. Co-teaching is not based on this premise. That is, co-teaching sometimes is used as a means for serving students with relatively mild needs. However, it also can be the option through which those with extensive needs are supported for at least part of the school day, as might be the case when students with significant disabilities participate in a co-taught class. How decisions about the appropriateness of co-teaching for particular students are made is a topic considered in Chapter 6.

Co-teaching is unique as a service delivery option in a second way. For students with disabilities, the other service approaches are outlined in federal special education legislation and have existed for many years in public schools. Co-teaching is not addressed in federal special education law, and it is relatively recent, a model existed 30 years ago but that that has evolved rapidly in schools over the past decade because of the growing expectation that students with disabilities should largely be educated in general education settings.

Professionally Licensed Educators Implement Co-Teaching

Which professionals participate in co-teaching depends on the characteristics of the students and the services to be offered. General education teachers, of course, are the first participants. However, they may co-teach with any other professional who brings needed, complementary expertise to the classroom, from special education teachers to reading specialists. The key is that the co-teachers are peers in terms of licensure and employment status. That is, they truly are colleagues who jointly make instructional decisions and share responsibility and accountability. Figure 1.1 summarizes the professionals most likely to join general educators to form co-teaching partnerships.

The individuals left out of this definition of co-teaching are paraprofessionals. Although these educators play critical roles in general education classrooms, their responsibilities are somewhat different. Appropriate roles of paraprofessionals are addressed later in this chapter.

Co-Teachers Share Instructional and Related Responsibilities

Have you ever heard co-teaching referred to as a professional marriage? In many ways (but not all), this metaphor is apt — co-teachers lead a classroom family, jointly establish their own culture, and negotiate their roles and responsibilities. They share successes and together solve problems that occur. However, co-teaching marriages are not all alike. Consider these two situations:

- In the first classroom, the marriage might seem like a caricature of the 1950s, 1960s, or 1970s... a professional version of an episode of *I Love Lucy, Leave it to Beaver, Happy Days,* or *The Brady Bunch.* The general education teacher clearly plays the role of instructional "dad," delivering the primary instruction, setting the classroom expectations, and taking full responsibility for ensuring that students are prepared for high stakes testing. The specialist takes on the role of instructional "mom." This person — even as a highly proficient professional — tends to be rather passive in the classroom, quietly redirecting students who are off-task and assisting students who did not understand the instruction that was delivered. Mom may believe that her role is to be a helper. If she believes that she should do more, she may feel like she does not have permission to proactively participate in classroom instructional and management decisions. That is, in this classroom, few conversations have occurred about professional roles; the teachers mostly are assuming traditional responsibilities — one teaching the overall group, the other ensuring that individual students receive remedial or other needed support.

- In the second classroom, the professional marriage is one from the twenty-first century. Roles and responsibilities are openly discussed and far fewer assumptions are made about the contributions that each educator should make. The specialist sometimes leads the science lab while the general educator ensures that all students are following the directions correctly. Sometimes the teachers divide the class in half and each one leads the same discussion so that all students have more opportunity to participate.

However, the special education teacher, ESL teacher, or reading specialist also sometimes works with struggling learners who are greatly helped by specially designed instruction, a careful and direct re-teaching of the material, or additional practice applying core skills. These teachers blend traditional and non-traditional roles and responsibilities. They constantly are on the alert to find new ways to combine their strengths to improve all students' learning.

Which type of marriage do you think is most likely to foster student success? It is the latter, of course. However, the first type of professional marriage is all too common. For co-teaching to have enough impact to improve outcomes for students, both teachers must have an unwavering commitment to the entire instructional process and actively contribute to helping all students reach their potential. Effective co-teaching relies on setting aside assumptions and engaging in an ongoing discussion of how to best utilize both professionals in the teaching and learning process.

All Students are Full Members of their Co-Taught Class

Do you or your colleagues divide students in your conversations, referring to "my students" or "your students?" Whenever this occurs, you are reinforcing an antiquated system, one that explicitly or implicitly communicates that learners with special needs are the responsibility of specialists, not general educators. It is crucial to remember that special education and other special services were designed to be *in addition to*, not *in lieu of*, general education. Thus, general education teachers are charged with teaching every student in the class, including those with disabilities or other special needs, and they are as accountable for their learning as they are for the learning of their other pupils. Co-teaching tends to bring issues such as this to the surface; how ownership of learners is discussed and addressed can have a significant impact on co-teaching success. Co-teaching is very much about OUR students.

Co-Teaching Occurs Primarily in a Single Shared Classroom

An assumption of co-teaching is that most instruction occurs with two educators working in the same physical space. This arrangement permits the educators to group and re-group students, draw on each other's expertise and energy, and revise and refine instruction as necessary. However, in some schools an informal agreement exists that when instruction seems difficult for learners with disabilities or other special needs, the students and "their" teacher should leave the classroom. If this occurs only occasionally it probably is not a problem, but if students leave the classroom several times each week, three concerns arise. First, for pupils with disabilities this may affect what is written on the individualized

Figure 1.1
Co-Teaching Applications

- **Special education teacher/general education teacher**

  This is the most common co-teaching arrangement. It has been part of special education services for more than 30 years for students with mild needs, those with behavior or emotional needs, and those with significant disabilities.

- **ESL teacher/general education teacher**

  This co-teaching arrangement has evolved over the past several years, especially with the expectation in federal legislation that English language learners will meet, after a relatively brief time, the same rigorous academic standards as other learners.

- **Speech-language therapist/general education teacher**

  This co-teaching arrangement is most common in elementary schools, especially in the primary grades. Typically, it may occur just once or twice each week in any single classroom, thus making it a challenging (but still effective and rewarding) option.

- **Media specialist/general education teacher**

  This co-teaching option usually is implemented for a unit, and it can be appropriate at any school level. The emphasis is on integrating appropriate literature into the instruction.

- **Literacy or math coach/general education teacher**

  When literacy and math coaches co-teach, they often use co-teaching as a way to model evidence-based instructional strategies and may do so to demonstrate a particular skill or for a time-limited period (e.g., one week for 30 minutes each day).

- **Gifted-talented educator / general education teacher**

  This co-teaching approach can be a means of integrating enrichment into general education classrooms. It also helps to ensure that students who may not otherwise access gifted/talented services can be incidental beneficiaries of them.

education program (IEP) in terms of time that is being spent in a general education setting and access to curriculum. For example, in a middle school with 85-minute block periods, two teachers decide that the students with disabilities should leave the class each day after 40 minutes. If the IEP indicates placement in the general education class, the arrangement is a significant violation of the IEP. In addition, if this occurs in a core academic class and the special education teacher is not highly qualified in that area, the student may not be receiving the access to curriculum promised in current federal law.

A second dilemma sometimes occurs with good intentions. If learners with disabilities need instruction in a separate setting, they certainly are entitled to it, and it should be reflected on the IEP. However, when this practice occurs, teachers sometimes have additional students leave the classroom. If the middle school teachers described above decided that two other struggling learners — who do not have IEPs — also should routinely leave for the remedial instruction, they are violating those students' rights. If the students have not been determined to be eligible for special education, they should not leave general education to receive what could be construed as special education services. This generally is true even if parents support the practice because federal and state laws clearly mandate a detailed, multidisciplinary assessment process and a team determination of eligibility and services for any student to receive special education.

A third dilemma concerns risks directly related to learning. That is, when some students leave a class, if one of the remaining students asks a question or the general education teacher re-explains a difficult concept, the pupils who left have missed potentially critical instruction. Even if teachers agree no new instruction will be delivered, it is very difficult to ensure that no new information or deeper discussions of academic content will occur.

These cautions should guide your general practice, but a few exceptions can be noted. For example, splitting students occasionally to accomplish an instructional purpose is appropriate (for example, having some students in the media center working on computers while others stay in the class to work on an assignment and then switching the groups the next day). In addition, your state department of education or school district may have specific policies about the situation in which a learner may be pulled from a co-taught class (and you should check with the appropriate administrator about this). In general, though, a fundamental question needs to be raised: If the aim in today's schools is to meet students' needs in general education, why not have as the primary pattern keeping these students there and providing support in that setting? Any service offered there is available to all learners and gives teachers many more options for meeting all student needs.

The Focus of Co-Teaching Is Access to the Curriculum

More than ever before, national attention is focused on raising the academic achievement of ALL students, including those with disabilities, those who are English language learners, those whose culture varies from that which usually characterizes U.S. schools, and those who are at a disadvantage because they live in poverty. Even for learners with significant intellectual disabilities who take alternate assessments, the goal is for there to be functional alignment with the general curriculum as might happen when a student learns just the vocabulary about safety related to electricity while others learn detailed concepts and vocabulary about it. The essential consideration is that co-teaching should not, in this day and age, ever be treated primarily or exclusively as a means for socialization. Although working on social skills might be a specific and very appropriate reason for a student with a disability or another special need to be in a co-taught class, it should not be the sole reason. An academic or pre-academic skill should also always be addressed.

Co-Teachers' Instructional Participation May Vary

The final element in defining co-teaching concerns participation. This topic affects professionals in secondary schools more than those in elementary schools. Many specialists have a background in elementary education or licensure in a single secondary subject area, and yet they may be asked to co-teach in several subjects or a subject which they have not had focused study. In these cases, it is particularly important to discuss what each person's contribution will be. The specialist may not deliver half the instruction, but some clear roles should be outlined. Could the specialist open the class with a brief review of material covered the day before? Take a lead in giving directions? Insert a vocabulary learning strategy into the instruction to be covered through a brief lecture? Co-teachers address this topic in hundreds of creative ways when it is pertinent. In fact, there is only one clearly unacceptable approach, and that is to have the specialist take a completely passive role during instruction until he or she "feels comfortable" with the material. Although that option might occur for a specific lesson, if it is a pattern, then the class is not co-taught, and the matter should be raised of whether it is worth having two teachers there.

Varying participation may, across all grade levels, also pertain to the chores related to teaching. If one specialist co-teaches in three or four classrooms per day, it is not realistic to expect that person to do half the preparation of materials. No formula can determine how chores should be divided, but this topic is covered in more detail in Chapter 3.

Before leaving the definition of co-teaching, a final word of clarification is in order. You may live in a state or district where alternative terminology is used. Your state might use *consultative teaching, collaborative teaching, integrated co-teaching, in-class resource services,* or another term to describe co-teaching. Such vocabulary differences will always exist, and it is not possible to address in one book all the variations that may be found. What is critical is that you understand the core concepts that underlie co-teaching so that you can recognize what it makes possible for students and realize the level of commitment that you need to ensure it succeeds.

What Co-Teaching Is Not

Many misconceptions about co-teaching exist. Consequently, many professionals are using the term *co-teaching* for such a wide variety of arrangements that it is as important to clarify what co-teaching is *not* as it is to clearly define it. Here are a few examples of what co-teaching is not:

- Co-teaching is not having an extra set of hands in the classroom. In co-teaching, *both* professionals are considered integral to the instructional process, and both have essential teaching roles.

- Co-teaching is not one person (usually the general education teacher) teaching while the other person (usually the specialist) roams around the classroom to provide assistance to students who need help with spelling, vocabulary, or task directions, or to address student behavior issues. Although providing assistance may be one component of a co-taught class, a topic addressed in Chapter 4, when one professional continually plays the role of the classroom assistant, the entire notion of an instructional partnership is undermined.

- Co-teaching is not an arrangement in which one person takes the lead teaching on Monday, the other on Tuesday, and first again on Wednesday, and so on. Variations of this misunderstanding are exchanging lead roles by week or by instructional unit. This type of turn-taking, usually a response to limited planning time, creates a classroom that has little more intensity than a class with one teacher because the richness of shared teaching often is lost. In this instance, the fact that each teacher leads does not eliminate the fact that one of the teachers typically is functioning as an assistant.

- Co-teaching is not a convenient means for busy educators to get non-teaching responsibilities completed. For example, although all professionals have emergencies that call them from the classroom and days when the duplicating just did not get completed, co-teaching should not be used as a mechanism for one professional to work on grading or make phone calls while the other teaches. The point of co-teaching is taking advantage of both professionals' knowledge and skills, and that requires that both teachers be present and full engaged in the teaching/learning process.

Co-Teaching and Related Terms

Too often in education, terms used to describe practices are not clearly delineated. Perhaps partly because co-teaching is not defined in law and is still evolving, it sometimes is given other labels that actually are about related — but different — concepts and activities. In this section, co-teaching is distinguished from three of the most commonly confused terms: collaboration, inclusion, and team teaching.

Collaboration

Did you think that the "co" in co-teaching stood for collaborative? Actually, it simply refers to the joint nature of this service delivery option. And although effective co-teaching includes collaboration, the two terms are not synonyms. Collaboration is a very broad term that refers to *how* professionals work together — in schools, or in any other endeavor, such as social services, business, and medicine. As Friend and Cook (2013) note, collaboration is a *style* for interaction that is based on

- mutual goals
- parity
- voluntariness
- shared responsibility for key decisions
- shared accountability for outcomes, and
- shared resources.

Further, collaboration is developmental, beginning with the belief by each participant that what is done together can be better than what each could do alone and including the growth of trust, respect, and a sense of community.

One straightforward way to illustrate collaboration is to think about a school situation such as this one: Two professionals have been told they are to co-teach during the upcoming school year. When they have a chance to meet, the general education teacher says, "I didn't agree to this; I was assigned. And I understand that you do not have much background in social studies. Since I'm the one responsible for the test scores in the class, I think it would be best if you did things that would help the kids but not interfere with the flow of instruction — take notes, make sure the kids are paying attention. Then when I finish, you can help your students if they need it." As you might guess, this diatribe is anything but collaborative. It uses a very directive style. The general education teacher has made it clear that she does not see a mutual goal, that her participation is not voluntary, that she will be in charge (thus undermining parity), and that decision-making and outcomes are not shared.

But what if the teacher had said this? "I didn't sign up for co-teaching and I'm not sure I even understand what we are supposed to be doing. But I suspect the administrators are counting on us to figure out how to make this work, so I'm willing to give it a try. How do you see two teachers working together in one classroom? One thing that I see we need to consider is how to fit your expertise on reaching students with special needs with my expertise in social studies. I'm anxious to hear your ideas and see what we can accomplish." The content and tone of this message is completely different. Even though the teacher was assigned to the teaching arrangement, working together is a choice she has made and exemplifies voluntariness. Further, the teacher is communicating the presence of shared goals, decision-making, and accountability. Respect has been communicated as have the beginnings of trust and a sense of community.

The strongest co-teaching is highly collaborative, but collaboration applies to many situations in addition to co-teaching (Cook & Friend, 2010). Middle schools teams should be collaborative, as should grade level teams in elementary schools and departments in high schools. Similarly, response-to-intervention (RTI) or multi-tiered systems of support (MTSS) teams rely on collaboration as do school leadership teams. If you remember that collaboration is a vehicle for accomplishing the work at hand, you'll understand that co-teaching is just one of many types of work enhanced by this interpersonal style.

Inclusion

In your school, are co-teaching and inclusion sometimes used as synonyms? Are classrooms where co-teaching is implemented called inclusion classrooms? Do staff members sometimes refer to "doing inclusion" (as in, "We do inclusion in the intermediate grades but not the primary grades," or "We do inclusion in the basic English class but not honors English") when what they mean is that they are implementing (or not implementing) co-teaching?

Distinguishing between the concepts of co-teaching and inclusion is critical because they are very different from each other. As noted earlier in this chapter, co-teaching is a service delivery option, a way to provide to students with disabilities or other special needs the specialized instruction to which they are entitled while ensuring that they can access the general curriculum in the least restrictive environment.

Inclusion is not a service delivery option. Inclusion is a belief system or philosophy that guides all the practices in any specific school. In fact, the smallest meaningful unit of inclusiveness is the school. There is no such thing as an inclusion class, an inclusion teacher, or — sadly — inclusion students. All these terms imply that inclusion is about where students sit during the school day. General education placement certainly is part of inclusive schooling, but it is just one dimension of it. In an inclusive school, all staff members believe that it is their job to provide the best education for all students, respecting their pupils' diversity and maximizing their potential. They believe that full participation with peers is the strong preference and make decisions that move away from general education placement only after thoughtful deliberation, but the goal is always membership in the same learning community. Highly inclusive schools have some pullout services available to students for whom it is necessary, but that pullout is guided by data-based decisions, revisited often, and continued only for as long as necessary. Conversely, in schools where professionals proclaim, "We're an inclusion school — we never pull any students out," it is unlikely that inclusive practices exist. In these schools, only a single means of addressing learners' needs is being used, and that is unlikely to be adequate.

How do inclusion and co-teaching fit together? Co-teaching as a service delivery option is one way that students in inclusive schools may receive their specialized education. But it is not the only way. As noted earlier in this chapter, some students may be served through consultation, that is, indirect services. Other students may receive some service in separate settings, either in combination with co-teaching or in place of it. The bias is always in favor of general education placement, but even more importantly, the needs of individual students are the first consideration.

Team Teaching

You may find that *co-teaching* and *team teaching* are sometimes used interchangeably, but two factors distinguish these terms and are reasons to understand their differences.

The first distinguishing feature of co-teaching versus team teaching concerns the number of students in the class group. Examples of team teaching throughout its lengthy history (for example, Warwick, 1971) typically have been characterized as keeping a constant teacher-student ratio. That is, when team teaching was introduced in the 1950s as a high school model called the Trump Plan (Friend, Reising, & Cook, 1993; Geen, 1985), it involved high school general education teachers combining multiple sections of a course so that one master teacher would deliver instruction, and then the other teachers would facilitate discussion and other class activities. When three teachers were involved, the arrangement would include approximately 75 students. Team teaching later was applied to elementary open-concept schools in which teams of approximately four teachers would share responsibility for teaching 100 students. Again, the teacher-student ratio was a constant. Even today, team teaching often is used in reference to middle schools where the 1-to-25 teacher-student ratio still is in place. It also sometimes describes high school courses that are interdisciplinary, such as an American studies class that teaches history through literature by blending a section of the history class with a section of a literature class so that the teachers can collaborate on instruction. But as in the other examples, the teacher-student ratio remains constant.

Co-teaching is very different. In co-teaching, the teacher-student ratio is dramatically reduced. That is, a class of 25 students with one teacher might be changed to a class of 25 students, five of whom have special needs, and two teachers for part or all of the school day. Changing the teacher-student ratio from 1:25 to 1:12.5 makes the classroom a more intensive teaching/learning environment, one that cannot be replicated in team teaching.

The second difference between co-teaching and team teaching concerns teacher expertise. In most of the professional literature that has addressed team teaching over the past five decades, it has been carried out by two general education teachers. On the other hand, co-teaching presumes that the two professionals have significantly different types of skills. This raises the question of each teacher's contribution. Here is one way to think about this.

General education teachers have these four areas of primary expertise:

1. **Curriculum and instruction.** General education teachers must hold knowledge of what needs to be taught, in what order, and how this content fits into the larger curriculum picture, including integration as appropriate with the Common Core State Standards (CCSS).

2. **Classroom management.** General education teachers always have relatively large class groups. They must be highly skilled at getting all the students focused, keeping them engaged, and doing this while addressing their various learning needs.

3. **Knowledge of typical students.** General educators have a good sense of whether student learning or social/behavioral functioning is within the parameters they expect. Although some teachers make errors in this arena, especially when students are from a cultural background other than theirs, general education teachers usually make sound judgments about whether students are simply struggling or may have a special need. One point is particularly important in this domain: Remember that general education

teachers are most likely to refer students for interventions and possible special education identification.

4. **Pacing.** General education teachers have to know how to get through the curriculum in the time allocated. Particularly in this age of accountability, this is an essential skill. They are vigilant to be sure that all essential skills for the grade level or subject are introduced to students so that they are prepared for high stakes testing and other assessments.

Of course, these are not the only skills that general educators possess, nor is it true that specialists do not have any of these skills. The point is that general educators, as a whole, have a specific set of prioritized knowledge and skills that are central to their role.

However, the same can be said for specialists, including special educators, ESL teachers, and others. Here are the four primary areas of expertise for them:

1. **Process of learning.** Whether a specialist works with young children or students about to leave high school and regardless of the specific special needs those students have, the goal of the professionals is to help their students learn how to learn. That is, they provide learners with strategies, accommodations, modifications, language instruction, or other interventions to facilitate learning, and they offer remediation or deliver specialized instruction.

2. **Individualization.** As professionals, specialists are trained to focus separately on each student and to design and deliver exactly what that student needs. This is especially true for students with disabilities: The Individuals with Disabilities Education Act (IDEA) has as its foundation this notion of individualizing, as embodied in the requirement that each student receiving special education must have an IEP.

3. **Documentation and other accountability paperwork.** Although all teachers complete paperwork, the burden for specialists tends to be more extensive than that for general education teachers. In addition, the documentation — whether IEPs, records of student language learning, other student records, test reports, record of parent contacts, and so on — can have legal ramifications, and so it must receive focused attention from these professionals.

4. **Emphasis on mastery versus coverage, with pacing as a secondary consideration.** Even in this era of increased accountability, specialists tend to prioritize helping students to truly master specific concepts and skills, even if it means not getting all the content that is supposed to be addressed. Their

rationale is that students whose understanding is incomplete are unlikely to be able to use the information and also unlikely to succeed in the next level of learning.

As was true in the discussion about general educators' skills, these are priorities. They are not the only skills that specialists possess, nor is it true that general educators have none of these skills.

Now the second difference between co-teaching and team teaching — the purpose for this entire discussion — can be highlighted. In team teaching, when two general educators with similar expertise and priorities work together, they usually share expectations. They worry about getting through the curriculum, raising achievement, and preparing students for high stakes testing, all appropriate and understandable goals. If two specialists taught together, they probably would spend considerable time addressing each student's special needs, documenting learning, and stressing mastery.

But consider what should happen when a specialist partners with a general education teacher. The differences in their professional orientation and expertise should lead to key differences in how each would approach instruction — and the result should be intense discussions, lively debates, and a classroom in which teaching and learning reflect the blended best of each perspective. That is, one teacher may want to speed up the pacing while the other expresses concern about the level of understanding of several students and volunteers to find some supplemental materials for them. One teacher may stress completing assignments independently while the other sees a need for coaching some learners and providing scaffolding for them. One teacher may set an expectation for all members of the class while the other teacher notes that one student is living in particularly difficult circumstances and needs special consideration.

Co-teachers sometimes will say, "You should see us in class. You can't tell us apart." If that means that both teachers are actively engaged in instruction, it is likely that the co-teaching is strong and facilitates student learning. However, if that comment implies that the teachers are, in essence, interchangeable, then the entire point of co-teaching is being missed. Teachers themselves should be comfortable and should instill the same comfort in students that co-teachers are *not* interchangeable. Each has a skill set and type of functioning that contributes to successful outcomes. This is especially true when you consider the fact that when this comment is made, it does not imply that both teachers function like specialists. Instead, it usually implies that both teachers appear to be general educators. What is needed in the classroom instead is clear implementation of the aspects of instruction in which each is an expert. Both teachers should always be active participants, occasionally they will appear to be functioning in the same way, but always they should be forging new types of instruction because of the unique strengths that each brings to the classroom.

Co-Teaching and Paraprofessionals

Professionals often ask how paraprofessionals fit into programs that emphasize co-teaching. The question is a valid one that should be addressed, but it also can be a slightly complicated one.

The straightforward answer is that paraprofessionals are valuable school personnel who provide support in the classroom, but they do not co-teach. Distinguishing what paraprofessionals do from what teachers do is essential.

Paraprofessionals who support students in general education settings can be asked to work with small groups of students, lead for selected students a review of concepts already taught, and assist a teacher in monitoring student attention, behavior, and work. However, they should not be asked to lead large-group instruction, plan and deliver initial instruction, interpret assessment results, make instructional decisions, or assume primary or sole responsibility for a group of learners over an extended period of time (e.g., Giangreco, Suter, & Doyle, 2010). In other words, they can support a classroom and may even carry out some activities that occur in co-teaching, but it is inappropriate to expect a paraprofessional to be a co-teacher. Further, although some paraprofessionals may hold current teaching licensure, professionals should keep in mind that their position descriptions still are more limited than the expectations typically set for teachers.

Similar comments could be made for classroom volunteers. When an individual is not employed as a licensed professional, co-teaching is not an option. Conversely, other licensed professionals, including speech/language therapists, psychologists, and counselors, can and sometimes do co-teach.

To keep all of this clear, some school staff members are beginning to use different terms for these two arrangements. *Co-teaching* is used to refer to arrangements in which licensed professionals are sharing in instructional delivery. *Supporting* is used to refer to situations in which a non-licensed individual (or individual employed in a non-license capacity) assists in a classroom.

Distinguishing the roles and responsibilities of paraprofessionals and specialists is not in any way intended to minimize the valuable assistance that paraprofessionals offer in the general education setting. Rather, it is to protect them from being asked to carry out, in essence, the job of a teacher — with nearly all parts of that job except the salary. At the same time, the distinctions are

Figure 1.2
Paraprofessionals in General Education: Examples of Tasks and Activities

- Re-read with students in a one-to-one arrangement stories or other materials after they have been introduced by a teacher.

- Review with students concepts they have not completely grasped after initial instruction, or provide additional practice to help students achieve mastery.

- Supervise students working independently so that the teacher is available to directly re-teach those who did not understand.

- Provide interpreting assistance as needed (for students who are ELLs).

- Maintain files related to students with disabilities, including portfolios being used for assessment purposes.

- Read aloud test items for students entitled to this option, following directions given by a teacher.

- Grade tests or other student work using a key or detailed rubric.

- Work with students in small groups that include typical learners for the purpose of fostering social interactions and facilitating learning.

- Prepare instructional materials needed for the class based on a sample or detailed directions provided by a teacher; assist in completing other chores.

- Provide personal assistance to students as needed, including moving students from place to place, helping with personal care, and so on.

- As directed by a teacher, collect and record data related to specific students or groups of students (for example, concerning behavior).

- Facilitate the use of assistive technology, which may include assisting the students to use equipment or software and reporting problems related to such items (for students with disabilities).

- Communicate to the specialist regarding matters directly related to students with special needs that may need teacher-teacher discussion.

intended to clarify that professionals should be actively involved in all aspects of the instructional process, that they should *not* be functioning like paraprofessionals. Figure 1.2 provides some examples of appropriate tasks and activities for paraprofessionals working in general education classrooms on behalf of students with special needs.

Entire books have been written about paraprofessionals. You should access such resources for detailed information if you work with these essential personnel. Keep in mind, though, that even if the paraprofessionals in your district or school are trained to carry out a remedial reading or math program, such instruction should be supplemental, as may occur with response to intervention (RTI) or multi-tiered systems of support (MTSS). Their work is not to take the place of that of teachers.

With an understanding of what co-teaching is and isn't, how several educational terms and concepts relate to co-teaching, and the role of paraprofessionals in supporting students and teachers, you have the background knowledge that is the basis for developing, refining, and sustaining an exemplary co-teaching program. Collaboration is the foundation for co-teaching since the ability to work together is integral to creating an effective co-taught class. In addition, fostering inclusive practices through collaboration creates a context in which co-teaching can thrive. Ultimately, supporting students with disabilities or other special needs through co-teaching can help educators to reach the goals of contemporary schools, that is, improving student achievement and reducing the gap between the outcomes for these students and their typical peers.

 For Further Thought

1. Which of the elements of the definition of co-teaching seems most critical to you? What steps could you, your co-teaching partner, and your principal take to ensure that co-teaching at your school incorporates each of these elements?

2. How do the explanations of co-teaching, collaboration, inclusion, and team teaching presented in this chapter compare to your previous understandings? How is each of these terms used in your school or district's policy documents or procedure manuals, IEP forms, and informal conversations? Why is it important to distinguish among them? What steps could be taken to align the concepts or terms with practices?

3. Analyze the unique contributions in co-teaching of general educators and specialists. How do these contributions fit you and your co-teachers? How do they vary depending on the specific specialist who is the co-teaching partner? Depending on the number of times per week that co-teaching occurs and for how long?

4. What is the role of paraprofessionals in providing support to students with special needs in your school? Which of the activities listed in Figure 1.2 do they carry out? What changes would you suggest to maximize their impact on student learning? What are the questions that general education teachers have concerning the work of paraprofessionals in their classrooms?

Taking Action

1. At a faculty, team, or department meeting, ask teachers to jot down their understandings of each of the terms presented in this chapter. Use their responses as the basis for a conversation about current practices in your school, the purpose for accurate use of the terms, and actions that could be taken to improve current practices.

2. Make a commitment to eliminate the divisive language of "my kids" and "your kids." For example, professionals could decide to assess a 25-cent fine against anyone who speaks in this way; the money could be given to charity at the end of the school year. Another idea is to encourage all staff members to say, "no, OUR kids" whenever the my/your language is used. Remember, when the language divides students the instructional practices are likely to do the same.

3. Create a brief questionnaire regarding co-teaching concepts and practices. Distribute it in order to gain an understanding of current practices and thinking in your school. For example, do co-teachers routinely have some students leave class? Do any of the examples of what co-teaching is NOT apply in your school? Are there questions you will seek answers for as you read the remainder of this handbook?

References

Cook, L., & Friend, M. (2010). The state of the art of collaboration in special education. *Journal of Educational & Psychological Consultation, 20,* 1-8.

Friend, M. & Cook, L. (2013). *Interactions: Collaboration skills for school professionals* (7th edition). Upper Saddle River, NJ: Pearson/Allyn & Bacon.

Friend, M., Cook, L., Hurley-Chamberlain, D., & Shamberger, C. (2010). Co-teaching: An illustration of the complexity of collaboration in special education. *Journal of Educational & Psychological Consultation, 20,* 9-27.

Friend, M., Reising, M., & Cook, L. (1993). Co-teaching: An overview of the past, a glimpse at the present, and considerations for the future. *Preventing School Failure, 37*(4), 6-10.

Geen, A. G. (1985). Team teaching in the secondary schools of England and Wales. *Educational Review 37,* 29-38.

Giangreco, M. F., Suter, J. C., & Doyle, M. (2010). Paraprofessionals in inclusive schools: A review of recent research. *Journal of Educational & Psychological Consultation, 20,* 41-57.

Honigsfeld, A., & Dove, M. G. (Eds.). (2012). *Co-teaching and other collaborative practices in the EFL/ESL classroom: Rationale, research, reflections, and recommendations.* Charlotte, NC: Information Age Publishing.

Isherwood, R., Barger-Anderson, R., Merhaut, J., Badgett, R., & Katsafanas, J. (2011). First year co-teaching: Disclosed through focus group and individual interviews. *Learning Disabilities: A Multidisciplinary Journal, 17,* 113-122.

Pardini, P. (2006). In one voice: Mainstream and ELL teachers work side-by-side in the classroom, teaching language through content. *Journal of Staff Development, 27*(4), 20-25.

Walsh, J. M. (2012). Co-teaching as a school system strategy for continuous improvement. *Preventing School Failure, 56*(1), 29-36.

Warwick, D. (1971). *Team teaching.* London: University of London.

Chapter 1 Appendix

The following section includes two activities that may help you, your co-teaching partners, and other colleagues to analyze your readiness for co-teaching and discuss your under-standing of how co-taught classes differ from those that are solo taught.

Co-Teaching and the Marriage Metaphor

Although the metaphor is not perfect, co-teaching has often been referred to as a professional marriage. Keeping that in mind, you can use the concept of personal relationships as a way of thinking about co-teaching partnerships. In the chart below (and possibly with colleagues), jot down ideas about the advantages and disadvantages of living alone. Then think about living with a spouse or significant other and repeat the exercise. Finally, apply your ideas to co-teaching. What do they tell you about developing a strong co-teaching partnership?

Living Alone

Advantages/Opportunities	Disadvantages/Limitations
1.	1.
2.	2.
3.	3.
4.	4.
5,	5.

Living Together

Advantages/Opportunities	Disadvantages/Limitations
1.	1.
2.	2.
3.	3.
4.	4.
5.	5.

Co-Teaching Applications

_____

_____

_____

_____

Co-Teaching Conversations

As you contemplate creating a co-teaching program or refining one that already exists, have you checked that all school staff members (and especially partners assigned to work together) share key understandings about co-teaching? Here are some questions that could be answered individually and then used as the basis for a team, department, or school-level conversation.

1. When you think about co-teaching, what is the picture of it that is in your head? That is, imagine a co-taught lesson. What do you see as your roles and actions? Those of your teaching partner? Those of the students?

2. If your school employs paraprofessionals, how would you distinguish between what two teachers in a classroom would be doing from what a teacher and a paraprofessional would be doing? How would an observer quickly notice the difference?

3. If your co-teaching pertains to both students with disabilities and those who are English language learners, what are the likely similarities and differences in what might occur in a co-taught class?

4. How do you think co-teaching balances the importance of students having curriculum access with tailoring instruction to meet their special needs?

5. After thinking about the key concepts related to co-teaching, what are your questions? What are your concerns about making co-teaching a success?

Chapter 2
The Rationale for Co-Teaching

*Far and away the best prize that life has to offer
is the chance to work hard at work worth doing.*

~ Theodore Roosevelt

Learner Objectives

1. Outline how education legislation and policy are fostering the implementation of co-teaching.

2. Analyze research that has examined the process and outcomes of co-teaching and use these studies to discuss the promise and problems of co-teaching as a viable service delivery option for students with disabilities and other special needs.

3. Discuss philosophical and anecdotal contributions to the rationale for co-teaching.

If your primary interest is in creating or refining your own co-teaching or in assisting your school or district to develop the best co-teaching program possible, you may not be particularly interested in reading about the rationale for co-teaching. You already know it is your goal, you do not sense any need to understand the details of why co-teaching is receiving so much attention, and you just want to get on with the many tasks you see ahead.

I hope, though, that you will take time to read the information contained in this chapter. There are several reasons for doing so. First, the information in this chapter can provide you with a bit of historical perspective on co-teaching as it has evolved, especially in special education, where it has a decades-long history. Second, the discussion of legislation related to co-teaching can give you information that might be useful to share with colleagues, parents/families, and community members. Third, a review of the research on co-teaching can assist you in understanding the empirical basis for this service delivery option and the types of questions that remain to be explored. Finally, the rationale for co-teaching has a philosophical and anecdotal dimension, and that perspective is given voice in this chapter.

If you are using this manual for a book study or in conjunction with a college class or project, you will find this background information helps to establish context for your emerging knowledge of the status of co-teaching. For individuals in this group, a bibliography of classic and contemporary resources on co-teaching, a few cited in this and other chapters, but many not, is included as the appendix for this chapter. I hope it helps you in your own pursuit of knowledge on this truly exciting option for educating students with disabilities and other special needs.

The Legislative Basis for Co-Teaching

From 1975 until 2001, educational practices for students with disabilities were guided by federal special education and civil rights laws, currently the *Individuals with Disabilities Education Act* (IDEA) of 2004 and Section 504 of the *Rehabilitation Act of 1973*. Whenever questions arose about the rights of these students and their families, the procedures through which decisions about their education were made, the strategies through which they would be assessed, or the services to which they were entitled, educators looked to IDEA or Section 504 and the many interpretations of them as clarified through litigation.

However, the reauthorization of the *Elementary and Secondary Education Act* (ESEA) in 2001 (also called the *No Child Left Behind Act*) drastically changed this approach. As you undoubtedly know, ESEA now mandates many of the most critical elements of educational practices for all students, including those with disabilities and other special needs, and when IDEA was reauthorized in 2004, its provisions were aligned with the broader law. ESEA requires that students be taught using methods that have been validated through research, includes nearly all students in mandated assessments, holds school districts accountable for the quality of the education students receive, and provides parents with options for ensuring that their children are able to reach the increasingly high achievement standards being set.

In the decade since ESEA and IDEA were enacted, a number of policy decisions at the federal and state levels also have profoundly affected educational practices. For example, the number of students considered eligible to take an assessment other than the one administered to typical learners has been further limited, and the goal for education has shifted from achieving adequate yearly progress to ensuring that students are college and career ready. In addition, most states have adopted the Common Core State Standards, which are intended to clarify for teachers, administrators, pupils, parents, and the community the essential knowledge and skills that students need to be prepared for success in our 21st-century society. Further, the evaluation of teachers in most locales now (or in the near future) is far more detailed and must directly incorporate a measure of student achievement in determining teacher effectiveness.

Together, current education legislation and policies have significantly raised expectations and focused attention on improving outcomes for all students, but especially those with disabilities and other special needs. As educators have grappled with the complex issues of how to operationalize all these various mandates, one solution adopted in many school districts is co-teaching. The following sections briefly describe how co-teaching is being used as a vehicle to implement school reform.

Access to the Curriculum

A fundamental aspect of both IDEA and ESEA is that all students have access to the same rigorous curriculum so that they can reach the high achievement expectations currently being set (e.g., Agran, Cavin, Wehmeyer, & Palmer, 2010; McLeskey & Waldron, 2011; Wassell, Hawrylak, & LaVan, 2010). Generally, this means that students with disabilities as well as those who are English language learners (ELLs) must meaningfully participate in the curriculum established by state and local policies for all students.

IDEA's traditional provision of educating students with disabilities in the last restrictive environment (LRE) is the basis for its attention to curriculum access for students with disabilities. This law further clarifies this matter by requiring that students' IEPs align with that curriculum and that, in most instances, general education teachers be part of the team that prepares the IEP.

Curriculum access is elaborated upon in other IDEA provisions as well. For example, students' progress in the curriculum must be recorded and communicated to parents at least as often as progress reporting is completed for other students (usually, each grading period). Federal special education law also mandates that supplementary aids and services be provided to students to facilitate their access to curriculum in the general education environment. In addition, it requires that the IEP team write a justification of any decision that removes a student from general education.

Collectively, the provisions of ESEA and IDEA and related policies communicate a higher standard than ever before that students with special needs should receive the same education as their peers. It is considered unacceptable practice for these students to miss out on learning the core curriculum or for educators to make decisions to eliminate parts of the curriculum or to substitute a simpler or functional-only curriculum. Because such curriculum access is seldom possible unless students are actually in the general education classroom, co-teaching is being implemented as a means to guarantee such access while simultaneously ensuring the delivery of the specialized instruction to which students are entitled.

Improved Academic Achievement

Access to the curriculum is not mandated simply so that students have exposure to it. A second component of current legislative and policy mandates is that access is for the purpose of improving academic achievement for students with disabilities and other special needs, closing the current gap between the outcomes for these students and the outcomes achieved by their peers without special needs.

In the past, students with disabilities as well as those who were English language learners might have been exempt from academic achievement testing, or their scores might have been separated from those of other students and not counted in considering a teacher's, school's, or district's effectiveness. This is no longer allowed. All students are to be assessed, their results must be reported, and all students' achievement scores are part of the equation for evaluating a school's instructional effectiveness. Even the scores of the one percent of students who complete an alternate assessment because they have significant intellectual disabilities are considered.

It should be noted that improved academic outcomes, while the focus of current efforts, are not the sole measure. The requirement of increased rigor also is measured in other ways. For example, under the provisions of IDEA all states (and hence, districts) now are paying attention more than ever before to the rate at which students with disabilities graduate from high school. Through response to intervention (RTI) or multi-tiered systems of support (MTSS), professionals also are carefully screening learners, especially in the early elementary grades, so that problems in achievement can be quickly identified and intensive interventions begun to accelerate learning and reduce or eliminate the identified learning gap before it becomes significant. Further, professionals are working to decrease the number of students who are suspended from school because every day that a student is out of school is a missed opportunity for learning.

All of the current mandates and initiatives related to student achievement have contributed to growth in co-teaching. Professionals have quickly realized that improving the academic outcomes of students with special needs is more likely to occur when general education teachers and specialists collaborate to embed in instruction in the core curriculum a wide range of tools that increase student attention and engagement, directly address their unique learning characteristics, and provide the increased instructional intensity necessary to reach achievement expectations (e.g., Sileo & van Garderen, 2010). This is far more readily accomplished through co-teaching than through systems that deliver special services in a separate setting with the expectation that professionals can effectively coordinate their efforts and students can transfer learning from the special setting to the general education setting. In addition, as professionals implement the Common Core State Standards, the importance of students learning with their typical peers with support provided by a specialist in that setting is likely to become even clearer.

Both for students with disabilities and those who are ELLs, it is important to note that this emphasis on academic achievement and the pressure it is creating for service delivery options such as co-teaching in no way is meant to infer that all instruction in a separate setting is inappropriate. Instead, this trend is emphasizing that accomplishing the goal of improving academic achievement is more feasible when students with special needs are educated alongside their peers without such needs. Further, it calls for educators to use instruction in a separate setting as a last resort and only to the extent that it leads to marked improvement in student learning. This topic is addressed in more detail later in this chapter.

Highly Qualified Teachers

A third component of both ESEA and IDEA concerns the necessity of all students being taught in the core curriculum by teachers who are highly qualified. The essence of this requirement makes sense: How could students possibly be meaningfully accessing the curriculum if their teachers are not determined to be qualified to provide it? However, like most of the current legislative and policy mandates, being highly qualified is a complex issue, and it has a number of dimensions. First, both special educators and ESL teachers generally must be highly qualified (based on state requirements and procedures) in their specialty areas. In addition, if they, by themselves, deliver core academic curriculum to students — such as teaching U.S. history in a separate setting, they also must be highly qualified in that core academic content area. However, even within this basic framework, there are variations. For example, special education teachers of students at the elementary age level and older students whose learning skills are at that level (that is, those with significant intellectual disabilities) usually must demonstrate that they have the knowledge and skills of elementary educators, or they are considered already highly qualified in that domain. ESL teachers in some locales are considered highly qualified to teach middle school or high school English because of their professional preparation in the ESL field.

In most states, one response to today's highly qualified requirements has been co-teaching. That is, this service delivery option can eliminate the dilemma of finding specialists who are highly qualified in both their own field as well as the core academic curriculum. For example, in the U.S. history example given above, if the course is co-taught, the general education teacher represents teacher qualification in social studies while the special educator represents qualification in the special education domain. Thus, the necessity of highly qualified instruction in both general education and special education for students with disabilities in the class is met. The same usually would be true for ESL teachers as well.

Keep in mind, though, the above provision does not hold in every state nor for all partnerships. For example, some state departments of education require that special educators hold highly qualified status in the core academic subjects in which they co-teach. A few have created a two-tier system: Co-teaching is reserved only for general educators with special educators who are highly qualified in both academic content and special education. A term such as "consultative teaching" is used when the special educator is not highly qualified, and in those instances, initial instruction is to be delivered only by the general educator. Further, it is likely that the strict requirements of highly qualified status may gradually be replaced by determination of "highly effective" status for teachers. What this might mean for co-teachers is not, at this point, clear.

A number of other variations of co-teaching policies can be found related to the matter of highly qualified teachers, and you should consider this brief overview just that, a sketch of the general requirements with examples to illustrate the complexity of this topic; it is not a comprehensive explanation. This is especially true since these requirements may change over time. If you have questions about being highly qualified, you definitely should ask an authoritative source in your state, possibly a university or state licensure official or a human resources staff member in your school district.

Current legislation and related policies, curriculum access, a focus on student academic achievement, and teachers' highly qualified requirements have had a significant impact on the education of students with disabilities, those who are English language learners, and others with special needs. In your district you may find that these changes have had a positive impact for students, but you also may find that they are creating challenges in providing specialized services that are difficult to overcome. In many school districts, though, co-teaching has become more common as a result.

Research on Co-Teaching

Much of what has been written about co-teaching consists of descriptions of successful and not-so-successful programs, suggestions for addressing the practical issues of establishing co-teaching programs, or advice on how to improve co-teaching arrangements. Over the past several years, though, a small body of research has slowly emerged that directly addresses various aspects of co-teaching. Although still limited in scope and depth, this scholarly work generally considers three aspects of co-teaching:

- Studies of the impact of co-teaching on student outcomes and studies addressing students' and parents' perceptions of it

- Studies of the relationships and practices employed by teachers in co-taught classes, and

- Studies of program structure and administration.

Because the overall purpose of this book is to assist educators in establishing and sustaining co-teaching programs, it is not possible to complete an exhaustive review of co-teaching research in this chapter. What follows are examples of the types of research being conducted and a brief discussion of how they are contributing to the evolution of co-teaching practices.

Co-Teaching and Students

If the primary goal of co-teaching is to ensure that students with disabilities or other special needs have access to the general education curriculum and can reach today's rigorous academic standards, you might think that most research about it would emphasize this topic. For many reasons, that is not the case. For example, to study whether co-teaching is more effective for students with disabilities or other special needs than a general education classroom with no co-teaching or a separate class covering comparable content or supplemental but related curriculum, many variables have to be controlled. Are the teachers teaching in approximately the same manner for the same length of time using similar strategies? Are the students in each group similar in terms of their abilities, needs, and backgrounds? Is the content comparable? Are assessments comparable and focused enough to discern what could be relatively small differences in student performance? Addressing all these factors makes it extraordinarily difficult to study co-teaching in a manner that would be considered rigorous in terms of research standards; consequently, few studies of this type can be found. An alternative is to use qualitative research methods that simultaneously consider many factors and identify patterns in the practices — but that usually do not compare class groups to one another.

Even studies that consider students' and families' perspectives on co-teaching are relatively rare. This may be the result of the newness of focused attention on co-teaching and a common pattern, at least in special education: Studies that explore student and family perceptions generally lag behind research on the implementation of new programs and services.

Here are examples of studies of co-teaching related to student outcomes and student and parent perceptions:

- Hang and Rabren (2009) studied 45 co-teachers (31 general educators and 14 special educators) whose students included 58 learners with disabilities (including learning disabilities, other health impairments, speech/language impairments, and five other disabilities) in grades 1 through 10. Data were gathered using a survey developed by the authors, observations in the co-taught classes, and a review of student records. The results obtained generally were positive: Students with disabilities in the co-taught classes improved significantly in terms of academic achievement when compared to the year prior to the study when no co-teaching occurred. Further, their achievement scores in reading, language arts, and math approximated those of all the students in their grade levels. Although all educators were positive about the impact of co-teaching on students, special educators even more than general educator reported that students received sufficient support to be successful in the co-taught environment.

  The authors of this study, however, also reported some puzzling findings. They found that student absences were higher during the co-teaching year than they had been during the prior year. In addition, students with disabilities had more discipline referrals in the co-taught setting, an unanticipated finding that may have been related to the fact that both teaching partners indicated that they were more responsible than the other for monitoring and responding to student behavior.

- Wilson and Michaels (2006) conducted a survey of students with disabilities and typical classmates who were enrolled in middle school and high school English classes. The survey included numerical ratings of various aspects of co-teaching as well as open-ended questions so that students would write about their perceptions. Both groups of students were favorable toward co-teaching. Students with disabilities recognized that co-teaching gave them access to the curriculum in a way not available in a special education setting, and they indicated that their skills had improved because of co-teaching. Typical classmates reported that co-teaching enabled them to develop higher levels of abstract thinking and enhanced their literacy skill development. Students also commented on aspects of co-teaching they did not like, including the fact that they could not work on homework from other classes because a teacher would quickly notice.

🧩 Walsh (2012) summarized data from Maryland school districts gathered over a 20-year span of co-teaching implementation and from one district over the past 6 years. The co-teaching was undertaken as a means of ensuring access to the general curriculum. He reported that students with disabilities who received their services through co-teaching had improved outcomes, including an accelerated rate of achievement on state-mandated reading and math tests. The data from that one county school district was used to demonstrate the efficacy of co-teaching as an instructional vehicle for students with disabilities.

🧩 Two large-scale evaluation studies provide a different type of student data related to co-teaching. Silverman, Hazelwood, and Cronin (2009) studied the characteristics of Ohio school districts that had demonstrated the greatest growth rate for the achievement of students with disabilities. They found the school districts shared several traits, including strong leadership and a collaborative culture. Co-teaching was found to be a primary service delivery model in those districts. More recently, Huberman, Naro, and Parrish (2012) examined the practices in four California districts that accomplished unusually strong academic performance for students with disabilities when compared to other districts. These researchers interviewed the special education directors and learned, among other findings, that the districts shared a strong commitment to inclusive education and access to the general curriculum as well as in-class and out-of-class collaboration between general and special educators.

🧩 Pardini (2006) is one of the only researchers who has studied co-teaching for English language learners. She reported on the experiences in the St. Paul, MN Public Schools in moving services for these students from separate settings to general education classes. With the largest populations of Somali and Hmong in the United States and a rapidly increasing Hispanic population, the district was offering ELL services in nearly every school in the district. The results of employing co-teaching were clear in the achievement data gathered: During 2003-2005, the time period covered by the report, the gap in reading achievement between other students and ELLs fell from 13 percent to 6 percent on high stakes testing; the gap in math fell from 6.7 percent to 2.7 percent. The results achieved by the district were among the best in the country for this student group.

Co-Teaching and Teachers

Most research related to co-teaching has addressed teacher perceptions of their partnerships, including their roles and the dilemmas they encounter related to those roles, and the ways in which the conduct their shared classes. Early studies on these topics tended to be very general, without any confirmation that the practices the teachers were using would be considered valid as co-teaching. More recent efforts often blend observation of the teachers with questionnaires and/or interviews. These studies capture more than any other type of research the complexity of co-teaching. Interestingly, most research of this sort has emphasized middle and high school partnerships. This is probably because the challenges of establishing co-teaching typically are perceived as much greater in secondary schools than in elementary schools.

- Harbort, Gunter, Hull, Brown, Venn, Wiley, and Wiley (2007) videotaped two high school science co-teaching teams and measured a variety of teaching and related behaviors using interval recording. They found that general educators presented instruction to students approximately 30 percent of the observation intervals; special educators did so for approximately 1 percent of the intervals. In contrast, special educators were observed "drifting"— walking around the room — slightly less that 50 percent of the intervals, far more than general educators. The authors discussed these results in terms of the importance of ensuring that instructional practices in co-taught classes are those most effective in improving student performance.

- Mastropieri, Scruggs, Graetz, Norland Gardizi, and McDuffie (2005) reported the results of four long-term qualitative case studies of co-teaching in science and social studies. Using interviews, observations, videotapes, and other data, they found a wide range of responses to co-teaching. For example, in some cases, co-teaching was seen as extremely effective in helping students with disabilities succeed in general education settings. In others, challenges such as the pressure that occurred related to high stakes testing limited student's access to co-teaching and its perceived success. One factor that strongly influenced classroom practices was the level of content knowledge of the special educator. Special educators generally did not have comparable knowledge of the subject matter; the researchers found that this tended to place them in the role of being an assistant while the general educator clearly was the lead teacher. The extent to which the teachers established a strong positive working relationship also was related to perceived co-teaching success.

- Keefe and Moore (2004) interviewed high school teachers to study their perceptions of co-teaching. They found that the teachers identified three themes that described their practices: (a) the nature of the collaboration; (b) the roles and responsibilities of the teachers; and (c) the outcomes for students. These professionals believed that co-teachers should have a voice in choosing their teaching partners, and they noted that teachers' ability to get along was a critical factor in co-teaching success. The professionals also indicated that direct conversations about roles and responsibilities in the classroom would have helped them avoid some problems, particularly the quandary of the special educator functioning more as a classroom assistant than a teaching partner. Like teachers in other studies, they mentioned the importance of content knowledge for special educators. Despite the difficulties encountered, these partners perceived co-teaching as positive for students with disabilities in terms of less stigma and higher achievement. None of these teachers reported negative outcomes from co-teaching, although special educators were concerned that decisions about students' services be made on an individual basis.

Co-Teaching Program Structure and Administration

Some researchers are interested in the ways in which co-teaching programs are structured, staffed, and administered. However, this type of information often is gathered as part of a larger study of teachers and students, or it is part of a study about overall inclusive practices, not just co-teaching. For example, in the Hazelwood et al. (2009) study mentioned above, making planning time available for collaboration was noted as a key element for improving student outcomes. This area of study is particularly important as school administrators plead for successful models. However, it is unlikely that research about program structure will every fully respond to this need because the way a program is structured and managed is dependent on many school-specific elements. It also should be noted that many of the studies considering administrative elements of co-teaching are dissertations; most of the available literature in journals on this topic is not research based. It consists primarily of program descriptions and advice.

Here are two studies that have directly examined programmatic and administrative matters related to co-teaching.

- Salisbury and McGregor (2002) examined the administrative climate and context of five successful inclusive elementary schools in three states. Using a school climate questionnaire, observations by on-site liaisons, and interviews with principals, they found several shared elements key to the schools' success. First, the principals of these schools were risk-takers who reflected on their actions. They were clear in their belief system and committed to making it a reality. In addition, they recognized the value of professional relationships, and they were accessible and willing to share decision making with staff members. Finally, these administrators were intentional — that is, they knew the goals they were working toward and used those goals to guide their work. They did not let obstacles divert their efforts; instead, they worked to overcome any challenges encountered.

🧩 Burnstein, Sears, Wilcoxen, Cabello, and Spagna (2004) looked at a school change model they implemented over a period of three years in two school districts moving toward inclusive practices. They interviewed administrators, teachers, and parents to gather data. Although their focus was not specifically co-teaching, their results help to inform co-teaching program development. They found that the schools in these districts implemented changes in very different ways: All became more inclusive, but some schools relied heavily on co-teaching, some kept a mix of traditional pullout and co-teaching practices but increased opportunities for students with disabilities to participate in general education classes, and some schools expanded inclusiveness to address the needs of students with significant disabilities. One significant conclusion was that all schools expressed as a priority keeping available an array of service options for meeting student needs.

If you have a conversation with any professional who is a student of research on co-teaching, you will hear that far more inquiry, including large-scale and rigorous studies, is sorely needed. An illustration of this state of affairs was found in a study by Müller, Friend, & Hurley-Chamberlain (2009). As they surveyed state department of education representatives to find out what types of data were being gathered at that level to inform policy and practice, they found the most common response was a request to obtain others' data! Perhaps with the continued pressure for school districts to gather and use data as the basis for decision-making, professionals will share empirical evidence regarding the accomplishments and dilemmas of co-teaching across settings and grade levels.

Philosophical and Anecdotal Evidence for Co-Teaching

Most of the philosophical and anecdotal information about co-teaching has come from the field of special education. For more than three decades and long before current federal education mandates, special educators were proposing that students with disabilities could succeed in general education classrooms if their teachers forged partnerships so that both high expectations and individualized support could be addressed there. As early as the 1980s (for example, Garvar & Parpania, 1982; Bauwens, Hourcade, & Friend, 1989), the concept of co-teaching was beginning to appear in the professional literature as an alternative to traditional, usually separate, special education special delivery models, one that conveyed optimism about the potential of blending the best of general education and special education (Epanchin & Friend, 2007; Friend, 2013).

Early writing about co-teaching reflected the growing trend of inclusive practices, and it represented a critical phase in the process of re-conceptualizing special education from being viewed as a *place* to being recognized as a *service*. Looking back, it should not have been surprising that this type of thinking would emerge. As early as the 1960s, Lloyd Dunn (1968) had questioned whether separate special education services were effective in improving outcomes for students with disabilities. His thinking was clearly incorporated in the least restrictive environment (LRE) provision of the 1975 Education of the Handicapped Act (Public Law 94-142, now IDEA), a provision still in place and already discussed earlier in this chapter as part of curriculum access. Dunn's thinking was re-iterated and extended in 1986 by Madeline Will, then Assistant Secretary of the U.S. Office of Special Education and Rehabilitation Services, when she called for a regular education initiative (REI) in which general and special educators would collaborate to educate students with disabilities along with their typical peers (Will, 1986).

The components of a rationale for co-teaching that came from this time period are still relevant today, and include (a) increased educational opportunities for all students; (b) less fragmentation in students' education; (c) a reduction in the stigma associated with being identified as having a disability or other special need; and (d) a stronger system of support among the adults responsible for educating students.

Increasing Educational Opportunities

The first part of the traditional rationale for co-teaching concerns the opportunities it creates for all students. That is, in co-taught classes the first concern is to provide to students with disabilities or other special needs options that otherwise would not exist. For students with mild to moderate disabilities this notion relates to learning the traditional curriculum. For students with significant disabilities this idea originally related to enhancing opportunities for interactions with typical classmates for the purpose of enhancing social skills. Today, of course, access to achieving academic goals are a key consideration. This same notion of increasing education opportunities now also is one of the factors leading to programs of co-teaching for students who are ELLs.

In a co-taught class, students who are gifted and talented should have more options for developing their extraordinary abilities. They should be able to demonstrate their mastery of the planned instruction and pursue their interests or add depth to their learning by extending their understandings. The presumption is that with two teachers, a place can be made in the instruction to move beyond what is intended for the majority of the learners. At least one study, outlined earlier, has supported this contention (Wilson & Michaels, 2006).

At the same time, students who struggle to learn but who are not eligible for special education or other specialized services also should be given the supports they need in order to succeed. Though clear data on this group of students have not been reported, many educators have expressed the perception that these at-risk learners are the ones who may reap the greatest incidental benefit from co-teaching. That is, the many strategies and techniques that special educators and ESL teachers know and use to enhance the learning of students with disabilities or those who are ELLs are just as effective for these students. In co-teaching, they receive the advantages of those strategies and techniques that would otherwise likely be unavailable to them.

Some educators also comment that a final group profiting from co-teaching includes average learners. These students may not require extraordinary attention, and so in a one-teacher classroom they may be overlooked. In co-teaching, though, the likelihood increases that they will be members of small learning groups, that they will have more opportunities to interact with the teachers, and that their less dramatic learning needs will be noticed and addressed.

Decreasing Educational Fragmentation

The second component of a traditional rationale for co-teaching concerns educational fragmentation and pertains in various forms to both elementary and secondary educational settings. In elementary schools, students who leave a general education setting to receive special education, related services, or ESL services typically miss small amounts of instructional time that may add up to be significant. That is, if a student spends a total of 12 minutes per day packing up, walking from one classroom to another, waiting for the specialist to be available to begin instruction, settling down, and then reversing this process at the end of the session, an hour per week of instructional time would be lost. The impact of moving students between settings is that those who need the most instructional time receive the least among all the students in a school. Co-teaching can eliminate this dilemma. Further, students have missed instruction while in the special education, related service, or ESL setting, and it can happen that no mechanism is in place to help them learn what was missed and connect the instruction presented in the specialized setting to that in the general education classroom.

For students in middle and high school, fragmentation relates to lost opportunities. That is, if students are assigned to receive special education services as part of their schedule, those services may be in lieu of courses that other students take. One example is foreign language, and the impact can be significant. If middle school students take Spanish but some students receive their special services instead, they are already significantly behind their peers when they reach high school. For a college-bound student with a disability or other special need, this may present a challenge that is very difficult to overcome.

The notion of lost instructional time and program fragmentation has changed somewhat with current legislation, especially because the highly qualified teacher requirement. This generally has led to less instruction in separate settings for middle and high school students. However, the issue is still important: When separate services are being considered, the costs of those services to the student's learning are as important to weigh as the benefits.

Reducing Stigma

Experienced educators know that some students, especially those in middle or high school, may dread being assigned to a special education or ESL class (even part-time) because of the stigma associated with it. The students may report that classmates call them names and that teachers presume they cannot learn, all because of their disability status or other labels and their participation in a separate education. One goal of co-teaching is to reduce or eliminate this stigma by making education seamless and the disability or language difference part of the learning variations that can be found in any classroom.

Of course, reducing stigma depends largely on the way in which co-teaching is implemented. If the special educator or ESL teacher in the general education classroom mostly hovers near the students with disabilities or ELLs to be sure they are paying attention, completing their work, and behaving appropriately, the stigma is increased instead of decreased. In contrast, if co-teachers use approaches such as those outlined in Chapter 4, stigma associated with labeling can largely be avoided.

Creating a Professional Support System

The final element of a philosophical and anecdotal rationale for co-teaching concerns professionals. Like most of the topics discussed in this section, few data exist to document the impact of this dimension of co-teaching, but it is important to mention nonetheless. For decades, teaching has been characterized as a lonely profession (Lortie, 1975), one in which isolation is the norm and collaboration is still not integral (Barth, 2006). This is gradually changing, and co-teaching can play a role in this shift in education culture (Friend & Cook, 2013; Honigsfeld & Dove, 2010). In fact, experienced co-teachers report that the camaraderie of a classroom partnership is energizing and comforting. That is, co-teachers relate that co-teaching helps them renew their commitment to teaching and inspires them to generate new ideas for reaching their students. They also comment that a teaching partner provides another important perspective on students, classroom procedures, instruction, and discipline.

Across the country, countless professionals have discussed how much they have learned from each other as a result of co-teaching. Many of them make comments like this one I recently heard from a high school English teacher: "I was reluctant to co-teach because I wasn't sure of what it would be like. Now I can't believe I was concerned. I really don't ever want to go back to doing nothing but teaching by myself." A special educator said this: "Sometimes I want to apologize to all the students I taught in my special education classroom. I had no idea what general education is like. Co-teaching is a whole different world. It's been hard for me to adjust, but it's the best thing that ever happened for kids. I've learned so much from my teaching partner and together we're really making a difference." These comments indicate that co-teaching opens for educators a world of classroom collaboration and all the many added possibilities that it brings for teaching diverse groups of learners.

 For Further Thought

1. How have you been personally affected by federal legislation and related policies regarding the education of students with disabilities, those who are English language learners, and those with other special needs? In what ways would you judge these laws successful in improving education for these students? Unsuccessful? Why?

2. As you review research related to co-teaching, what does it suggest to you are the most critical elements of it? If you were to make one change in your own co-teaching on the basis of the research you reviewed, what would that change be?

3. Would you consider co-teaching a valid, research-based practice at this time? Why or why not? What other research do you think the field should undertake in order to clarify the impact of co-teaching on student outcomes? What other student variables should be studied?

4. How important are the traditional aspects of a rationale for co-teaching, those that originated in the early days of inclusive practices? How might you use information about the philosophical and anecdotal reasons for co-teaching to explain its importance to your administrator or to a group of concerned parents?

Taking Action

1. With your colleagues, design a study that you could complete related to co-teaching at your school. You might use one of the studies reviewed in this chapter as a model, or you could design another type of action research project. Base your research on a critical question for which you believe an answer would improve co-teaching practices. One strongly recommended area of study is the impact of co-teaching on student performance on high-stakes and other achievement measures. Other areas to explore could include student social interactions, discipline referrals, or student perception of their two-teacher class.

2. Have all the professionals in your school or at least those participating in co-teaching select articles to read from the bibliography in this chapter's appendix or from other sources. Over several sessions or at department or faculty meetings, have individuals summarize what they have read and offer ideas about the implications of the information for their own classrooms and the school's program, making sure to distinguish practices that are research-based from those that are based on perceptions and opinions.

References

Agran, M., Cavin, M., Wehmeyer, M., & Palmer, S. (2010). Promoting active engagement in the general education classroom and access to the general education curriculum for students with cognitive disabilities. *Education and Training in Autism and Developmental Disabilities, 45,* 163-174.

Barth, R. (2006). Improving relationships within the school house. *Educational Leadership, 63*(6), 8-13.

Bauwens, J., Hourcade, J.J., & Friend, M. (1989). Cooperative teaching: A model for general and special education integration. *Remedial and Special Education, 10*(2), 17-22.

Burnstein, N., Sears, S., Wilcoxen, A., Cabello, B., & Spagna, M. (2004). Moving toward inclusive practices. *Remedial and Special Education, 25,* 104-116.

Dunn, L.M. (1968). Special education for the mildly retarded — is much of it justifiable? *Exceptional Children, 35,* 5-22.

Epanchin, B.C., & Friend, M. (2007). The adolescence of inclusive practices: Building bridges through collaboration. In J. McLeskey (Ed.), *Reflections on inclusion: Classic articles that shaped our thinking.* Arlington, VA: Council for Exceptional Children.

Friend, M. (2013). Inclusive practices. In J. A. Banks (Ed.), *Encyclopedia of diversity in education* (pp. 1144-1147). Thousand Oaks, CA: Sage.

Friend, M., & Cook, L. (2013). *Interactions: Collaboration skills for school professionals* (7th edition). Upper Saddle River, NJ: Pearson/ Merrill.

Garvar, A.G., & Papania, A. (1982). Team teaching: It works for the student. *Academic Therapy, 18,* 191-196.

Hang, Q., & Rabren, K. (2009). An examination of co-teaching: Perspectives and efficacy indicators. *Remedial and Special Education, 30,* 259-268.

Harbort, G., Gunter, P. L., Hull, K., Brown, Q., Venn, M. L., Wiley, L. P., & Wiley, E. W. (2007). Behaviors of teachers in co-taught classes in a secondary school. *Teacher Education and Special Education, 30,* 13-23.

Honigsfeld, A., & Dove, M. G. (2010). *Collaboration and co-teaching: Strategies for English learners.* Thousand Oaks, CA: Corwin.

Huberman, M., Navo, M., & Parrish, T. (2012). Effective practices in high performing districts serving students in special education. *Journal of Special Education Leadership, 25*(2), 59-71.

Keefe, E.B., Moore, V., & Duff, F. (2004). The four "knows" of collaborative teaming. *Teaching Exceptional Children, 36*(6), 36-42.

Lortie, D. (1975). *Schoolteacher: A sociological study.* Chicago: University of Chicago Press.

Mastropieri, M.A., Scruggs, T.E., Graetz, J., Norland, J., Gardizi, W., & McDuffie, K. (2005). Case studies in co-teaching in the content areas: Successes, failures, and challenges. *Intervention in School and Clinic, 40,* 260-270.

McLeskey, J., & Waldron, N. L. (2011). Educational programs for elementary students with learning disabilities: Can they be both effective and inclusive? *Learning Disabilities Research & Practice, 26,* 48-57.

Müller, E., Friend, M., & Hurley-Chamberlain, D. (2009, May). State-level approaches to co-teaching. *inForum* [policy analysis], pp. 1-7. Available from http://www.projectforum.org.

Pardini, P. (2006). In one voice: Mainstream and ELL teachers work side-by-side in the classroom teaching language through content. *Journal of Staff Development, 27*(4), 20-25.

Rea, P., McLaughlin, V.L., & Walther-Thomas, C.S. (2002). Outcomes for students with learning disabilities in inclusive and pullout programs. *Exceptional Children, 68,* 203-222.

Salisbury, C., & McGregor, G. (2002). The administrative climate and context of inclusive elementary schools. *Exceptional Children, 68,* 259-270.

Sileo, J., & van Garderen, D. (2010). Creating optimal opportunities to learn mathematics: Blending co-teaching structures with research-based practices. *Teaching Exceptional Children, 42*(3), 14-21.

Silverman, S. K., Hazelwood, C., & Cronin, P. (2009). *Universal education: Principles and practices for advancing achievement of students with disabilities.* Columbus, OH: Ohio Department of Education, Office for Exceptional Children.

Walsh, J. M. (2012). Co-teaching as a school system strategy for continuous improvement. *Preventing School Failure, 56*(1), 29-36.

Wassell, B. A., Hawrylak, M., & LaVan, S. (2010). Examining the structures that impact English language learners' agency in urban high schools: Resources and roadblocks in the classroom. *Education and Urban Society, 42,* 599-619.

Will, M.C. (1986). Educating children with learning problems: A shared responsibility. *Exceptional Children, 53,* 411-415.

Wilson, G.L., & Michaels, C.A. (2006). General and special education students' perceptions of co-teaching: Implications for secondary-level literacy instruction. *Reading & Writing Quarterly, 22,* 205-225.

Chapter 2 Appendix

This appendix is a listing of many references and resources related to co-teaching. Some of the articles, chapters, and books have a research base, but others do not. These resources are not intended to be comprehensive. Instead they are provided to give you a sense of the array of materials available and the topics they emphasize.

Selected Bibliography on Co-Teaching

Historical Perspectives

Adams, L., & Cessna, K. (1991). Designing systems to facilitate collaboration: Collective wisdom from Colorado. *Preventing School Failure, 35*(4), 37-42.

Adams, L., Tolman, P., Cessna, K., & Friend, M. (1995). *Co-teaching: Lessons from practitioners.* Unpublished manuscript, Colorado Department of Education, Denver.

Armbruster, B., & Howe, C.E. (1985). Educators team up to help students learn. *NASSP Bulletin, 69*(479), 82-86.

Bauwens, J., Hourcade, J.J., & Friend, M. (1989). Cooperative teaching: A model for general and special education integration. *Remedial and Special Education, 10*(2), 17-22.

Epanchin, B.C., & Friend, M. (2008). The adolescence of inclusive practices: Building bridges through collaboration. In J. McLeskey (Ed.), *Classic articles about inclusion.* Arlington, VA: Council for Exceptional Children.

Friend, M., Reising, M., & Cook, L. (1993). Co-teaching: An overview of the past, a glimpse at the present, and considerations for the future. *Preventing School Failure, 37*(4), 6-10.

Garver, A.G., & Papania, A. (1982). Team teaching: It works for the students. *Academic Therapy, 18*, 191-196.

Geen, A.G. (1985). Team teaching in the secondary schools of England and Wales. *Educational Review 37*, 29-38.

Warwick, D. (1971). *Team teaching.* London: University of London.

Research on Co-Teaching

Austin, V.L. (2001). Teacher's beliefs about co-teaching. *Remedial and Special Education, 22*, 245-255.

Conderman, G., & Stephens, J.T. (2000). Reflections from beginning special educators. *Teaching Exceptional Children, 33*(1), 16-21.

Conderman, G., & Johnston-Rodriguez, S. (2009). Beginning teachers' views of their collaborative roles. *Preventing School Failure, 53*, 235–244.

Dieker, L. (2001). What are the characteristics of "effective" middle and high school co-taught teams for students with disabilities? *Preventing School Failure, 46*, 14-23.

Eisenman, L. T., Pleet, A. M., Wandry, D., & McGinley, V. (2011). Voices of special education teachers in an inclusive high school: Redefining responsibilities. *Remedial and Special Education, 32*, 91-104.

Foley, R.M. (2001). Professional development needs of secondary school principals of collaborative-based service delivery models. *High School Journal, 85*(1), 10-23.

Gurgur, H., & Uzuner, Y. (2010). A phenomenological analysis of the views on co-teaching applications in the inclusion classroom. *Educational Sciences: Theory and Practice, 10*(1), 311–331.

Hang, Q., & Rabren, K. (2009). An examination of co-teaching: Perspectives and efficacy indicators. *Remedial and Special Education, 30,* 259–268.

Harbort, G., Gunter, P. L., Hull, K., Brown, Q., Venn, M. L., Wiley, L. P., & Wiley, E. W. (2007). Behaviors of teachers in co-taught classes in a secondary school. *Teacher Education and Special Education, 30,* 13-23.

Hasan Gurgur & Yildiz Uzuner (2011). Examining the implementation of two co-teaching models: Team teaching and station teaching. *International Journal of Inclusive Education, 15,* 589-610.

McDuffie, K. A., Mastropieri, M. A., & Scruggs, T. E. (2011). Differential effects of peer tutoring in co-taught classes: Results for content learning and student-teacher interactions. *Exceptional Children, 75,* 493-510.

Huberman, M., Navo, M., & Parrish, T. (2012). Effective practices in high performing districts serving students in special education. *Journal of Special Education Leadership, 25*(2), 59-71.

Idol, L. (2006). Toward inclusion of special education students in general education: A program evaluation of eight schools. *Remedial and Special Education, 27,* 77-94.

Isherwood, R., Barger-Anderson, R., Merhaut, J., Badgett, R., & Katsafanas, J. (2011). First year co-teaching: Disclosed through focus group and individual interviews. *Learning Disabilities: A Multidisciplinary Journal, 17,* 113-122.

Magiera, K., Smith, C., Zigmond, N., & Gebaner, K. (2005). Benefits of co-teaching in secondary mathematics classes. *Teaching Exceptional Children, 37*(3), 20-24.

Malone, D., & Gallagher, P. A. (2010). Special education teachers' attitudes and perceptions of teamwork. *Remedial and Special Education, 31,* 330–342.

Mastropieri, M.A., Scruggs, T.E., Graetz, J., Norland, J., Gardizi, W., & McDuffie, K. (2005). Case studies in co-teaching in the content areas: Successes, failures, and challenges. *Intervention in School and Clinic, 40,* 260-270.

Murawski, W., & Swanson, H. (2001). A meta-analysis of co-teaching research: Where are the data? *Remedial and Special Education, 22,* 258-267.

Murray, C. (2004). Clarifying collaborative roles in urban high schools: General educators' perspectives. *Teaching Exceptional Children, 36*(5), 44-51.

Pardini, P. (2006). In one voice: Mainstream and ELL teachers work side-by-side in the classroom teaching language through content. *Journal of Staff Development, 27*(4), 20-25.

Pearl, C., Dieker, L., & Kirkpatrick, R. (2012). A five-year retrospective on the Arkansas Department of Education co-teaching project. *Professional Development In Education, 38,* 571-587.

Rytivaara, A., & Kershner, R. (2012). Co-teaching as a context for teachers' professional learning and joint knowledge construction. *Teaching and Teacher Education: An International Journal of Research and Studies, 28,* 999-1008.

Scruggs, T. E., Mastropieri, M. A., & McDuffie, K. A. (2007). Co-teaching in inclusive classrooms: A metasynthesis of qualitative research. *Exceptional Children, 73,* 392-416.

Wallace, T., Anderson, A.R., & Bartholomay, T. (2002). Collaboration: An element associated with the success of four inclusive high schools. *Journal of Educational and Psychological Consultation, 13,* 349-381.

Walsh, J. M. (2012). Co-teaching as a school system strategy for continuous improvement. *Preventing School Failure, 56*(1), 29-36.

Wasburn, Moses, L. (2005). Roles and responsibilities of secondary special education teachers in an age of reform. *Remedial and Special Education 26,* 151-158.

Weiss, M.P. & Lloyd, J. (2002). Congruence between roles and actions of secondary special educators in co-taught and special education settings. *Journal of Special Education, 36,* 58-68.

Wilson, G.L., & Michaels, C.A. (2006). General and special education students' perceptions of co-teaching: Implications for secondary-level literary instruction. *Reading and Writing Quarterly, 22,* 205-225.

Zigmond, N. (2006). Reading and writing in co-taught secondary school social studies classrooms: A reality check. *Reading and Writing Quarterly, 22,* 249-268.

Books and Other Resources

Beninghof, A. M. (2012). *Co-teaching that works: Structures and strategies for maximizing student learning.* San Francisco, CA: Jossey-Bass.

Chapman, C., & Hyatt, C. H. (2011). *Critical conversations in co-teaching: a problem-solving approach.* Bloomington, IN: Solution Tree Press.

Conderman, G. J., Bresnahan, M. V., & Pedersen, T. (2009). *Purposeful co-teaching: Real cases and effective strategies.* Thousand Oaks, CA: Corwin.

Dieker, L. (2007). *Demystifying secondary inclusion: Powerful school-wide and classroom strategies.* Port Chester, NY: Dude Publishing.

Friend, M. & Cook, L. (2013). *Interactions: Collaboration skills for school professionals* (7th edition). Upper Saddle River, NJ: Pearson/Allyn & Bacon.

Friend, M., & Bursuck, W.D. (2012). *Including students with special needs: A practical guide for classroom teachers* (6th edition). Upper Saddle River, NJ: Pearson/Merrill.

Friend, M., Burrello, L., & Burrello, J. (2009). *More power: Effective instruction in co-taught classes* [videotape]. Bloomington, IN: Forum on Education, Indiana University.

Friend, M., Burrello, L., & Burrello, J. (2004). *Power of Two* (2nd edition) [videotape]. Bloomington, IN: Forum on Education, Indiana University.

Honigsfeld, A., & Dove, M. G. (Eds.). (2012). *Coteaching and other collaborative practices in the EFL/ESL classroom: Rationale, research, reflections, and recommendations.* Charlotte, NC: Information Age Publishing.

Honigsfeld, A., & Dove, M. G. (2010). *Collaboration and co-teaching: Strategies for English learners.* Thousand Oaks, CA: Corwin.

Perez, K. (2012). *The co-teaching book of lists.* San Francisco, CA: Jossey-Bass.

Chapter 3
The Co-Teaching Partnership

The strength of the team is each individual member.
The strength of each member is the team.
~Phil Jackson

Learner Objectives

1. Explain the importance of a shared philosophy, prerequisite skills, and collaboration in forming strong and effective co-teaching partnerships.

2. Analyze topics that co-teachers should address in order to strengthen their partnership and avoid miscommunication.

3. Discuss matters related to classroom procedures and behavior management that co-teachers may need to negotiate in their co-taught class.

The practice of co-teaching is based on creating and refining a strong professional relationship with your partner. Although for some teachers this may be a simple matter, for many others and for a wide variety of reasons it requires careful attention, negotiation on critical classroom issues, and persistence (Friend & Cook, 2013).

Many factors contribute to achieving a strong co-teaching partnership. First, co-teachers should address fundamentals such as the prerequisites each educator brings to the instructional context, their shared belief system, and their understanding of how they will collaborate. A second set of factors comprise topics related to specific situations, tasks, and activities related to teaching (e.g., dividing responsibilities, correcting teacher errors). Finally, co-teachers typically should clarify classroom procedures and behavior management strategies. They may share similar perspectives on some aspects of setting up, teaching in, and efficiently managing a shared class, but they may differ on others.

Some of the topics addressed in this chapter may be inconsequential for you and your co-teacher. Others may be significant. One point this chapter makes is that, just like in the marriage relationship that co-teaching often is compared to (e.g., Kohler-Evans, 2006), clear communication is essential (Gately & Gately, 2001). Some co-teachers may chuckle to think others worry about some of the matters raised here, but they also may find some of these topics are ones that they have found bothersome. If none of the topics seem pertinent to you, it may be that you and your partner have considerable experience and have already worked out the professional relationship. However, it could also mean that you should more carefully analyze your co-teaching and explore several of the topics outlined to see if you could strengthen it. Also keep in mind that as you co-teach, discussing areas of concern soon after they are noticed can prevent small disagreements from becoming serious problems that interfere with your shared instructional effectiveness.

The Foundation of an Effective Co-Teaching Partnership

During the early 1990s, an extensive research project was undertaken in Colorado to capture essential elements of co-teaching (Adams, Cessna, & Friend, 1993). Interviewing many pairs of experienced co-teachers and following up on that initial research with a detailed study of successful and unsuccessful co-teaching partnerships, the researchers found that five key components must be in place, components that have been validated repeatedly and still are central to effective co-teaching. Three of these components concern the professional relationship and are briefly described in this section. The other two (that is, classroom practice and administrative support) are considered in Chapters 4 and 6. In the appendix that follows this chapter you will find the *Colorado Assessment of Co-Teaching* (Co-ACT), based on this research, which can assist you in reflecting on your current and ideal co-teaching relationships and practices. It is most useful as a tool for discussing the topics it addresses and is not intended as an evaluation instrument.

Co-Teaching Prerequisites

Even before co-teaching begins, prerequisites that each educator brings to the classroom should be recognized as affecting it. Experienced co-teachers report that these are the most important prerequisites:

1. **Personal prerequisites.** Co-teachers should have personal qualities that are supportive of working with colleagues. For example, they need a sense of humor and a willingness to set aside differences once they have been addressed. The most important prerequisite, though, is likely to be the ability to give up control. Teachers by nature tend to be rather controlling. For working with students, this is a positive attribute. However, other adults do not like to be controlled, and co-teachers need to be sure that this potential source of conflict is directly addressed (Conderman, 2011). Even teachers who think they are not controlling should ask their co-teachers about this issue and take any feedback to heart.

2. **General professional prerequisites.** Co-teachers need to understand school, teaching, and students. Although not common, when a teacher does not understand the educational process and culture, problems can occur. One example concerns a young special educator who tended to function as a friend to students instead of as a teacher. That is, he would joke around with students until they became boisterous and then suddenly get angry at them for misbehaving. Despite feedback, coaching, and professional development he could not seem to understand that his role as a teacher differed from the role of buddy. He clearly was not ready to co-teach. Occasionally, understanding school is related to culture. Some teachers acculturated to educational systems outside the U.S., for example, may expect a level of obedience and deference not typical among U.S. students and may respond harshly if challenged.

3. **Discipline-specific prerequisites.** Finally, co-teachers must possess the specialized expertise that forms the reason for the partnership. General educators should be expert in the four areas mentioned in Chapter 1, and special educators, ESL teachers, and other specialists should be expert in their four areas. Although all educators learn from each other through co-teaching and usually become better educators because of it, co-teaching is premised on participants having a firm grounding in their own areas of knowledge and skill.

Shared Philosophy

Effective co-teachers have a shared philosophy of teaching and learning, one that reflects their priorities and beliefs. This shared philosophy needs to extend beyond general statements such as "All children can learn" and "The job of teachers is to take students from where they are as far as they can go." Instead, the shared philosophy is more about the core beliefs that each teacher has about the ways that teaching and learning should occur, student behavior, and professionals' responsibilities. For example, one teacher may believe that assignments changed for any student should carry a minor grade penalty. The other teacher may argue that when changes are made to accommodate special needs, no differences should be made in grading. What are the other examples of differences in beliefs that could affect co-teaching? Co-teachers are likely to agree about most of their beliefs, but any differences should be noted, discussed, and possibly negotiated in terms of expectations for students. The key is to make sure that co-teachers' overall goals are consistent and that their communication is clear. Their differences should be considered a strength, but shared core beliefs are foundational for co-teaching.

Directly related to philosophy is a personal commitment to co-teaching. Recall from Chapter 1 the examples of interactions between co-teachers, one in which the general education partner was resistant and said so, relegating the specialist to the role of helper, and one in which the general educator expressed uncertainty but also a willingness to work with the specialist. A different type of example also could be used. The specialist may regularly make to the general education teacher one of these two comments: "I'll listen while you teach and take notes and help the students who don't seem to understand," or "Even though I'm not completely confident of this content, I'm sure we can find a way to make this effective." Across these examples, unless both educators demonstrate that they believe in this instructional arrangement, they are not likely to make it succeed. Of course, it's not just words — it's also actions. For example, general educators demonstrate commitment by sharing lesson plans in advance and inviting the specialist to provide input on those plans and the related activities. Specialists demonstrate commitment by initiating conversations about strategies that could be embedded in the lessons to reach learners with special needs as well as contributing to the chores of teaching.

Collaborative Relationship

In Chapter 1, collaboration was distinguished from co-teaching. However, experienced co-teachers stress that co-teaching truly is a collaborative relationship and, as such, it depends on sharing goals for students, sharing responsibility for key decisions and accountability for outcomes, and sharing resources — the very characteristics of collaboration already introduced (Friend, Cook, Hurley-Chamberlain, & Shamberger, 2010). They also note that co-teaching requires the development of trust and respect and a sense of classroom community (Tannock, 2009). Even for co-teachers who intuitively understand the potential of this service delivery option and who enthusiastically implement it, collaboration is developmental. That is, it grows stronger and matures over time.

Collaboration has intuitive appeal, but it sometimes is a challenge in co-teaching (Cook & Friend, 2010; Sims, 2008; Wasburn-Moses, 2005). For example, consider what occasionally happens when two veteran teachers are partnered. Each of these professionals is accustomed to a particular teaching approach, a set of procedures for facilitating the teaching/learning process, and a strategy for managing the classroom and related chores. These teachers typically problem solve with automaticity, that is, they recognize and resolve classroom and student issues without needing to consciously consider each decision made. When such teachers are partnered, they may find that co-teaching interferes with automaticity, that is, when another professional is present it is necessary to take into account that person's views and preferences. The result can be that co-teaching feels particularly awkward for veteran educators. It is especially important that they recognize the source of the discomfort, learn to discuss it in a constructive way, and negotiate with their partners to address related issues that arise (e.g., Chapman & Hyatt, 2011). Eventually, veteran professionals acquire a new type of automaticity, one that includes the procedures of co-teaching.

Other Topics Concerning the Partnership's Foundation

_____

_____

_____

_____

Strengthening the Co-Teaching Partnership

An essential extension of the foundational components of a co-teaching relationship is dialogue about specific topics that operationalize those key components and strengthen the partnership. By directly discussing matters such as the examples in the following paragraphs, professionals can avoid miscommunication, empower each other, and thus enrich student learning.

Parity in the Classroom

How will you communicate to each other, to students, and to parents that you and your teaching partner have equivalent expertise and truly share responsibility in the classroom? This topic is related to the description of collaboration presented in Chapter 1 (Friend & Cook, 2013). At the elementary level, parity may relate to who begins instruction or gives permission for students to leave the classroom. In middle and high school, parity may be directly related to who stands at the front of the classroom during instruction and who grades student work. In yet other classrooms, parity is related to having two workspaces that are equivalent (rather than having the specialist assigned to a student desk or table) and making sure that co-teaching begins on the first day of school, with both teachers immediately taking an active role in instruction. Remember that special, ESL, and general education teachers have different types of expertise. The goal is to find ways to blend them to enhance student learning (Murray, 2004). Some common and essential indicators of parity are included in a checklist in the appendix that follows this chapter, and attention to them can enhance your partnership. Are there others that you would add?

Division of Labor for Teaching and Related Responsibilities

In some schools, general education teachers express concern that special educators go from room to room without any specific obligations to be active participants in the teaching process and all the many tasks it requires. Although it is not reasonable to expect specialists who co-teach in several classes to share half the teaching tasks in each one, co-teachers should discuss which teaching responsibilities could be shared or how the preparation of materials could be divided.

Preferences for Out-of-Class Communication

Co-teachers who spend the day together have ongoing opportunities to discuss their instruction and students. However, in a large school in which co-teachers may not see each other except during their co-teaching time, they may need to discuss their preferred communication options and strategies to make communication most effective and efficient. For example, email may be viewed as the optimum strategy because it can be stored on a computer. However, e-mail has drawbacks as well, and other alternatives, such as a wiki (discussed in Chapter 6), might be more effective and efficient. Likewise, text messages are quick, but they are best for small matters, not detailed planning. A few teachers prefer a face-to-face meeting after school or a phone call in the evening, but both teachers have to agree to this primary communication mode.

Strategies for Responding to Mistakes that Occur During Teaching

Have you ever realized that you made an error in your teaching or had your students point out that you had made a mistake? Perhaps when adding 29 and 48 and you wrote 67 on the board. Or you may have misspelled the word perseverance as *perserverence.* You quickly corrected it and moved on because errors are part of teaching. However, teachers sometimes worry about how to respectfully tell their co-teachers during the teaching process about an error, especially when the partners are teaching in an area in which they both have limited experience or the professional relationship is somewhat tenuous and a correction could be perceived negatively. This topic can be easily addressed before the problem arises. Some teachers might agree that the person who notices the mistake will just correct it without saying anything. Other professionals might want to use signal words in a class. They agree that if one person says, "I'd like to rephrase that," it means there has been an error that needs correcting. The specific strategy for addressing errors is not the issue — it's having a respectful way to do so that has been decided upon in advance.

Preferences for Receiving Feedback

Most professionals are self-aware, knowing that they respond best when they receive feedback in a certain manner. Perhaps they want to be sure that any debriefing occurs the same day as a lesson, or perhaps they would like to wait until the next day to discuss anything that occurred. Most professionals would prefer that any discussion about a disagreement on teaching procedures, responses to students, or other topics be completed in private (not the teacher's lounge) and with respect. You may find that you never need to follow the strategy you and your colleague develop for exchanging feedback, but if a need arises the plan is in place. One difficult aspect of co-teaching for some professionals is initiating a discussion of topics where disagreement exists. One teacher might use cynicism in talking to students and it bothers the other teacher. One teacher may not consistently implement the classroom behavior management plan, and this frustrates the other. Finding ways to hold these conversations decreases the later occurrence of more serious problems and enhances collaboration (Friend & Cook, 2013).

Maintenance of Confidentiality

Teachers know that information about students must be kept confidential, and the same is true for co-teachers. However, they may have to be particularly careful on this matter because of their shared work. They may discuss students as they walk down the hall together or eat lunch at school or stand in line at a local fast food restaurant. Their concern and commitment is admirable — but inadvertently violating confidentiality through such conversations must be avoided. A second type of confidentiality also must be considered: Co-teachers should avoid discussing the co-taught class unless both teachers are present. This simple strategy can eliminate miscommunication and misunderstanding.

Acknowledgment of Pet Peeves

All teachers have pet peeves. These may relate to students (for example, pen-tapping, tilting a chair back, addressing a teacher by saying "Hey" instead of using the teacher's name), teachers (for example, borrowing pens or pencils, getting materials or supplies out and not putting them back), or any aspect of teaching and learning (for example, duplicated materials that are not clear, dirty computer keyboards). Co-teachers are advised to touch base with each other about their pet peeves. Discussing them, even if the items that concern one teacher are very different from those of the other, ensures that miscommunication is avoided. For example, if one teacher does not want students to go to lockers for any reason after the bell rings, the other teacher (who is not as adamant on this point) can follow the partner's wishes.

Other Topics Concerning Partnership

_____

_____

_____

_____

Classroom and Behavior Management

In addition to exploring other topics, co-teachers should spend a few moments clarifying their expectations regarding classroom procedures and behavior management. By directly conversing about these domains, potential conflict about expectations can be avoided.

Use of Space for Instruction

Many of the co-teaching approaches outlined in Chapter 4 include simultaneous instruction of multiple groups of students. For the students in the groups to be able to focus their attention, complete their own work, and avoid disrupting others' work, teachers need to analyze their physical space and identify ways to use it for maximum effectiveness. They might decide that a low bookcase now against a wall would serve as an effective sight and sound barrier if placed at a right angle to the wall. They could decide, since their classroom has whiteboards on two opposing walls, that parallel teaching can best be managed by having half the students face one board while the other half faces the opposite direction. The goal is to think about space use and take into account the potential for student and teacher focus or distraction when two teachers work together.

Tolerance for Noise and Strategies for Keeping Noise at an Acceptable Level

Co-teachers may wish to discuss each person's tolerance for noise in the classroom when several activities are occurring simultaneously. Many of the most effective co-taught classrooms would sound raucous to a guest, but the clamor is purposeful. To manage noise, both teachers should instruct students to speak in low voices, and they also have to remind themselves and each other to do the same. Teachers also should discuss where each person should stand or sit during instruction. For example, in parallel teaching, teachers might want to sit during instruction if they face each other across the room. Otherwise their voices may carry to the other side. If noise seems to bother a student, the teachers may want to find a desk carrel for the student or provide a single desk tucked into a quiet corner of the classroom for that student to use. If either teacher is bothered by the classroom noise level, the topic should be added to the agenda for the next shared planning session so that options to resolve this dilemma can be discussed.

Organizational Routines

This topic concerns all the details of classroom operation. What do students do with assignments as they are completed? What are acceptable activities for them to do if they complete work before the end of the lesson? Do students need to ask permission to go to the restroom or simply pick up a hall pass and leave? How do students line up to leave the classroom? May students pack up before the bell rings? You can probably list at least another dozen procedures that are part of day-to-day classroom life. Special educators or other specialists who are in any single classroom for only a short time generally follow the procedures established by the general education teacher — they just try to be aware of what those procedures are. If co-teachers are together all day or even half of each day (a pattern in some elementary schools and a handful of secondary schools, as discussed in Chapter 7), then more negotiation on classroom procedures might be in order. Also, if some students cannot follow typical class procedures — as could happen for a student with autism, for example — the specialist should make recommendations for addressing the student's needs.

Procedures for Substitute Teachers

Co-teachers sometimes discuss what will happen in the class when a substitute teacher is necessary. As with many of the topics mentioned in this chapter, no single answer is recommended for integrating substitute teachers into co-teaching. Some teachers ask the substitute teacher to assume a helping role because the remaining partner knows the instruction that comes next and can manage the class. If a co-teacher will be absent for an extended time, a decision about the responsibilities of the substitute teacher may depend on that person's experience in the classroom and skills related to the subject area, special education, or ESL program.

Safety Procedures

Co-teachers should discuss general safety procedures, including those related to evacuating the school in case of fire, taking shelter in case of tornadoes or earthquakes, or responding to any other type of school emergency. Both teachers should know where to go and how to access any supplies kept in the classroom. In addition, co-teachers should be sure that both know whether any students need special consideration in case of an emergency. For example, the fire alarm may badly frighten a student who wears hearing aids, and a student with limited English skills may need to be assigned a partner who can guide him in an emergency situation. Similarly, the teachers should know what procedure to follow in case of a fire (when elevators are not accessible) for students with physical limitations whose classes are on the second floor.

Classroom Rules

Co-teachers should check that they agree on the rules established for the shared classroom. If schoolwide positive behavior supports are in place, the expectations set for classrooms should be acceptable. However, if your school leaves the matter of rules to each teacher, this can be an important topic. One teacher may post rules and consequences that are mostly negative (for example, do not leave your seat unless given permission: first consequence is moving your name from the green circle to the yellow and the second consequence is moving to red and losing minutes of recess). The other teacher may strongly prefer a system based on positive consequences (for example, treat your materials and those of others with respect; each student earns "cash" for appropriate behavior that is used once every two weeks to purchase privileges or tangible rewards). A discussion may help to address this topic as well as a related one — that is, the extent to which rules are enforced consistently.

Discipline Procedures for Specific Students

Even if all organizational procedures are clarified and classroom discipline addressed, some students with disabilities will need further accommodations. A student with ADHD may need a standing desk (similar to a lectern) so that he can move as he works. A student with a learning disability may need a contract through which she earns rewards for each 10 minutes of on-task behavior. General education teachers may not be aware of the requirement of these kinds of individualized behavior supports, and special educators should ensure that they are provided as outlined by the IEP or determined to be necessary as an informal form of support for the student.

Other Topics Concerning Classroom and Behavior Management

_____

_____

_____

_____

As you can see from the various topics covered in this chapter, developing a strong co-teaching partnership relies on addressing broad philosophical beliefs as well as the nuts and bolts of sharing a classroom and teaching together (Ploessl, Rock, Schoenfeld, & Blanks, 2010). That is, co-teachers should prioritize finding time to ensure that their shared classroom efforts have a strong foundation. The conversations that co-teachers have in order to analyze their non-negotiables, preferences, expectations, and assumptions about teaching and learning are central to creating solid programs that quickly develop into strong partnerships producing improved outcomes for students. To continue your own conversation, complete the activity in the appendix concerning what each partner brings to co-teaching.

For Further Thought

1. Of the topics related to the foundation of strong co-teaching partnerships, which do you find the most important? Why? Those mentioned were originally identified some 20 years ago. Why do you think they continue to be so central to co-teaching?

2. What topics would you add to the list of classroom and teaching items that should be discussed by co-teachers? How does your list compare to the list prepared by your teaching partner?

3. When you think about classroom procedures and behavior management, what are your priorities? How do your priorities compare with those of your co-teacher? What changes could be made to your preferences in order to take into account both professionals' perspectives?

Taking Action

1. Consider using professional development opportunities at your school to refine professionals' collaboration skills. Through book study, speakers, video, or other means, learn more about how to raise and discuss difficult or awkward matters, ask questions and make statements in ways that enhance communication, increase awareness of nonverbal communication, respond to resistance, effectively communicate with parents — even when disagreements occur, and negotiate. Skills for collaboration enhance co-teaching partnerships, a specialized application of collaboration.

2. Begin working on a list of non-negotiables for your school's co-teaching program. What items should be on the list for all co-teachers? Find a place to post a draft list and continue to refine it so that expectations are clearly articulated. Discuss how these non-negotiables should be part of your teacher evaluation system.

References

Adams, L., Cessna, K., & Friend, M. (1993). *Co-teaching feasibility study.* Denver, CO: Colorado Department of Education, Special Education Section.

Chapman, C., & Hyatt, C. H. (2011). *Critical conversations in co-teaching: A problem-solving approach.* Bloomington, IN: Solution Tree Press.

Conderman, G. (2011). Methods for addressing conflict in co-taught classrooms. *Intervention in School and Clinic, 46,* 221-229.

Cook, L., & Friend, M. (2010). The state of the art of collaboration in special education. *Journal of Educational & Psychological Consultation, 20,* 1-8.

Friend, M., & Cook, L. (2013). *Interactions: Collaboration skills for school professionals* (7th edition). Upper Saddle River, NJ: Pearson/Allyn & Bacon.

Friend, M., Cook, L., Hurley-Chamberlain, D., & Shamberger, C. (2010). Co-teaching: An Illustration of the complexity of collaboration in special education. *Journal of Educational & Psychological Consultation, 20,* 9-27.

Gately, S.E., & Gately, F.J. (2001). Understanding co-teaching components. *Teaching Exceptional Children, 33*(4), 40-47.

Kohler-Evans, P. A. (2006). Co-teaching: How to make this marriage work in front of the kids. *Education, 127,* 260-264.

Murray, C. (2004). Clarifying collaborative roles in urban high schools: General educators' perspectives. *Teaching Exceptional Children, 36*(5), 44-51.

Ploessl, D. M., Rock, M. L., Schoenfeld, N., & Blanks, B. (2010). On the same page: Practical techniques to enhance co-teaching interactions. *Intervention in School and Clinic, 45,* 158-168.

Sims, E. (2008). Sharing command of the co-teaching ship: How to play nicely with others. *English Journal, 97*(5), 58-63.

Tannock, M. T. (2009). Tangible and intangible elements of collaborative teaching. *Intervention in School and Clinic, 44,* 173-178.

Wasburn-Moses, L. (2005). Roles and responsibilities of secondary special education teachers in an age of reform. *Remedial and Special Education, 26,* 151-158.

Chapter 3 Appendix

The first item in this appendix is an adaptation of the Colorado Assessment of Co-Teaching (CO-ACT), a research-based instrument drawing from the essential components of co-teaching introduced in Chapter 1 and presented in more detail in this chapter. It considers co-teachers' working relationships, the use of two professionals in the classroom, and the structure and preparation for the co-teaching program. The remaining appendix pages provide an exercise for having a meaningful conversation between co-teachers concerning what each person contributes to the partnership and a checklist for assessing parity in the classroom.

Colorado Assessment of Co-Teaching (CO-ACT)

Co-teaching occurs when two educators jointly deliver instruction to a group of students primarily in one classroom. One form of co-teaching is when general and special educators teach in a classroom that includes some students who have identified disabilities.

This instrument is designed to help you understand the critical components of successful general-special education co-teaching. The items included do not encompass everything about co-teaching. Instead, these are co-teaching elements that have been found to differentiate exemplary from other co-teaching teams.[1]

If you are a co-teaching novice, responding to this questionnaire can help you prepare for your new role and responsibilities. If you are a veteran co-teacher, you may use this to reflect on and refine your skills. Co-teaching partners will find it especially helpful to discuss their responses.

Although the CO-ACT was developed for special educators, the concepts and practices it addresses are largely universal. If you are co-teaching as part of an ESL program, if you slight adjust the wording (for example, thinking about individual learning plans (ILPs) instead of IEPs), you will find it is applicable to your partnership.

NOTE: This instrument was developed as part of a federally funded project when co-teaching was a relatively new concept. It is based on extensive interviews with experienced co-teachers. In fact, the items largely come directly from co-teachers' descriptions of their practices. Once developed, the instrument was validated through what is called a known-groups study. That is, co-teachers nominated by their supervisors as (a) exemplary or (b) struggling completed the survey. The participants did not know they had been rated as exemplary or struggling. When their data were analyzed through a factor analysis, certain items clearly distinguished between the two groups. Those are the only items included in this final form of the survey, with the exception of the four items in Factors IV and V, which are explained in the scoring section. Since its original development, the CO-ACT has been used in several dissertations as a means of determining the quality of co-teaching implementation and as a vehicle for assisting co-teachers to reflect on their practices.

[1] We wish to acknowledge the co-teachers in Colorado who participated in the research that led to the development of this instrument.

ANALYZING YOUR CO-TEACHING

For each of the following items that describe successful co-teaching, respond in two ways. Rate the **importance** of each statement by checking responses on the scale to the left. Also, rate the **extent to which the item is present** by checking responses on the scale to the right.

How much do you agree that each factor is important in co-teaching

How much do you agree that each factor describes your co-teaching situation?

Personal Prerequisites

#	Statement	IMPORTANCE: strongly disagree	disagree	neutral	agree	strongly agree	PRESENCE: strongly disagree	disagree	neutral	agree	strongly agree
1.	Co-teachers are willing to share their knowledge and skills with each other.	1	2	3	4	5	1	2	3	4	5
2.	Co-teachers monitor student progress on a regular basis.	1	2	3	4	5	1	2	3	4	5
3.	Co-teachers monitor student progress in all areas of the curriculum.	1	2	3	4	5	1	2	3	4	5
4.	The general education teacher has skills to teach the curriculum effectively.	1	2	3	4	5	1	2	3	4	5
5.	Co-teachers regularly assess what's working and what isn't.	1	2	3	4	5	1	2	3	4	5
6.	Co-teachers are confident of their skills as individual teachers.	1	2	3	4	5	1	2	3	4	5
7.	Co-teachers are competent problem solvers.	1	2	3	4	5	1	2	3	4	5
8.	One of the general education teacher's strengths is knowledge of the curriculum.	1	2	3	4	5	1	2	3	4	5
9.	Co-teachers make a commitment to deliberately build and maintain their professional relationship.	1	2	3	4	5	1	2	3	4	5
10.	Co-teachers each have a distinct but essential purpose in the co-taught class.	1	2	3	4	5	1	2	3	4	5
11.	Co-teachers make a unique contribution based on — but not limited to — their professional expertise.	1	2	3	4	5	1	2	3	4	5
12.	Co-teachers vary student grouping arrangements to foster student learning.	1	2	3	4	5	1	2	3	4	5
13.	Students in a co-taught class receive help and structure to complete assignments.	1	2	3	4	5	1	2	3	4	5
14.	Co-teachers model effective communication.	1	2	3	4	5	1	2	3	4	5
15.	Co-teachers model cooperation.	1	2	3	4	5	1	2	3	4	5

How much do you agree that each factor is important in co-teaching

How much do you agree that each factor describes your co-teaching situation?

IMPORTANCE						PRESENCE				
strongly disagree	disagree	neutral	agree	strongly agree		strongly disagree	disagree	neutral	agree	strongly agree
					The Professional Relationship					
1	2	3	4	5	16. Co-teachers are able to release some control to their co-teacher.	1	2	3	4	5
1	2	3	4	5	17. Co-teachers are equally responsible for what happens in the classroom	1	2	3	4	5
1	2	3	4	5	18. Co-teachers make important decisions together.	1	2	3	4	5
1	2	3	4	5	19. Co-teachers carry their part of the workload.	1	2	3	4	5
1	2	3	4	5	20. During a lesson co-teachers can sense the others' thoughts and direction.	1	2	3	4	5
1	2	3	4	5	21. Co-teachers share the gentle and the tough roles.	1	2	3	4	5
1	2	3	4	5	22. One co-teacher can pick up where the other left off.	1	2	3	4	5
1	2	3	4	5	23. Co-teachers monitor on-task behavior during instruction.	1	2	3	4	5
1	2	3	4	5	24. Co-teachers are organized.	1	2	3	4	5
					Classroom Dynamics					
1	2	3	4	5	25. Co-teachers switch instructional strategies when necessary.	1	2	3	4	5
1	2	3	4	5	26. Co-teachers make continual adjustments to ensure student success.	1	2	3	4	5
1	2	3	4	5	27. Co-teachers adapt assessment tools and procedures as needed.	1	2	3	4	5
1	2	3	4	5	28. Co-teachers use a variety of techniques to motivate students.	1	2	3	4	5
1	2	3	4	5	29. In a co-taught class students may be working on the same goal, but they may demonstrate their accomplishment in different ways.	1	2	3	4	5
1	2	3	4	5	30. The curriculum in a co-taught class includes social-emotional skills.	1	2	3	4	5
1	2	3	4	5	31. The special educator has skills to develop and adapt curricula to meet the unique student needs.	1	2	3	4	5
1	2	3	4	5	32. Co-teachers know a variety of ways to respond to student diversity.	1	2	3	4	5
1	2	3	4	5	33. Co-teachers believe students' needs determine classroom practice.	1	2	3	4	5
1	2	3	4	5	34. Co-teachers believe it's important to balance academic needs of students.	1	2	3	4	5

PRESENCE

How much do you agree that each factor
describes your co-teaching situation?

How much do you agree that each factor is
important in co-teaching

IMPORTANCE

strongly disagree	disagree	neutral	agree	strongly agree		strongly disagree	Disagree	neutral	agree	strongly agree
					Classroom Dynamics (continued)					
1	2	3	4	5	35. Co-teachers believe co-teaching is worth the effort.	1	2	3	4	5
1	2	3	4	5	36. Co-teachers share a philosophy about learning and teaching.	1	2	3	4	5
1	2	3	4	5	37. Co-teachers believe their purpose is to facilitate learning as well as to impart knowledge.	1	2	3	4	5
1	2	3	4	5	38. The special educator has skills to suggest instructional strategies to meet unique student needs.	1	2	3	4	5
					Contextual Factors					
1	2	3	4	5	39. Co-teachers regularly set aside a time to communicate.	1	2	3	4	5
1	2	3	4	5	40. Co-teachers have schedules that permit them to plan together.	1	2	3	4	5
					Universal Elements					
1	2	3	4	5	41. Co-teachers trust each other.	1	2	3	4	5
1	2	3	4	5	42. Co-teachers respect each other's professionalism.	1	2	3	4	5

SCORING INSTRUCTIONS To provide additional information about your responses, we suggest you analyze them in this way. Add the scores you gave each item in Factors I, II, and III (Factors IV and V are explained below) for all of the items. Write the total for each factor in the appropriate blank.

Importance		Presence	
Factor I	_____	Factor I	_____
Factor II	_____	Factor II	_____
Factor III	_____	Factor III	_____
Total	_____	Total	_____

Add down the columns to determine the instrument total.

UNDERSTANDING YOUR SCORES This section contains a description of each of the factors and information on the average scores obtained by exemplary teams. It is intended to help you understand your responses. Notice how exemplary co-teachers rated their own practices as exceeding their ratings of the importance of each item

Factor I: Personal Prerequisites. Personal prerequisites are the skills and characteristics that each teacher brings to a co-teaching situation. They include your teaching style, knowledge specific to your discipline or subject, and your contribution to the classroom. The average total scores of exemplary co-teaching teams on this is: Importance - 66.16 Presence - 68.03

Factor II: The Professional Relationship. The professional relationship describes the collaborative interaction of the co-teachers. It includes the sense of parity between co-teachers, the ability to work toward a shared goal, and the extent to which key decisions are shared, and accountability for those decisions. The average total score of exemplary co-teaching teams on this factor is: Importance - 37.28 Presence - 38.69

Factor III: Classroom Dynamics. Classroom dynamics are the beliefs and actions that give added benefit to the co-taught classroom. These include your perceptions of how teaching and learning occur, your knowledge of the academic and social curriculum, and the rage of individualizing strategies you use. The average total score of exemplary co-teaching teams on this factor is: Importance - 60.88 Presence - 62.75

Factor IV: Contextual Factors. Contextual factors include the temporal conditions that facilitate co-teaching. Only two items were identified as critical by the teachers who validated this instrument. Both items suggest the importance of allocating time for shared planning. Because there are only two items in this factor there is no score to report as for the other factors.

Factor V: Factor V items are slightly different than the others. This factor consists of items that form the foundation of co-teaching. The two items in this category were rated as **highly important** by all the co-teachers who participated in the original co-teaching study. While the "presence" scores did not discriminate highly effective teams from others, the two statements were rated so highly important that we included them in the instrument for your consideration.

Total score. One additional way of considering your responses on the instrument is to look at your total score. When you consider this score, it is important to keep in mind that co-teaching has many variations. A high overall score typically reflects co-teaching that relies extensively on a collaborative relationship. While teachers report that highly collaborative co-teaching is very fulfilling for them and very beneficial for students, because of circumstances it may not be the most preferred or feasible type for you. Other less intensive approaches to co-teaching can also be effective. The average total score of exemplary co-teaching teams is: Importance - 163.92 Presence - 169.08

Parity, Parity, Parity

How do you and your co-teaching partner convey to students that your teaching relationship is truly collaborative, that it is a partnership based on parity? The following checklist might help you to think through ideas about how you, your teaching partner, and students can observe parity (or its absence). NOTE: Do keep in mind that which of the following parity signals pertain to your situation depends on many factors.

Already do	Should do	Not applicable	
_____	_____	_____	1. Both teachers' names are on the board or posted in the classroom.
_____	_____	_____	2. Both teachers' names are on schedules and report cards.
_____	_____	_____	3. Both teachers' handwriting is on student assignments (that is, the specialist at least occasionally grades a set of papers).
_____	_____	_____	4. Both teachers have space for personal belongings.
_____	_____	_____	5. Both teachers have similar furniture (i.e. desks, chairs).
_____	_____	_____	6. Both teachers sometimes take a lead role in the classroom.
_____	_____	_____	7. Teacher talk during instruction is approximately equal.
_____	_____	_____	8. Both teachers give directions or permission without checking with the other teacher.
_____	_____	_____	9. Both teachers work with all students
_____	_____	_____	10. Both teachers are considered teachers by students.

My Contributions to Our Co-Teaching Partnership

Co-teachers should reflect on what they contribute to the partnership. This can help novices understand that co-teaching is not about the two educators being the same but rather valuing what each contributes. Similarly, it can help veterans review how well they are taking advantage of each person's expertise.

Respond to the following questions regarding your contributions to co-teaching, using information from Chapter 1 and this chapter, and jotting your responses in the chart below:

1. What are the strengths you bring to a co-teaching partnership? Think about qualities you have as a person, your knowledge as an educator, and specialized skills you may have related to your specific area of expertise.

2. What are the liabilities that you bring to a co-teaching partnership? Think about your personal characteristics, challenges you would face regardless of your professional role, and those within your discipline and across disciplines.

My Strengths for Co-Teaching	My Liabilities for Co-Teaching
1.	1.
2.	2.
3.	3.
4.	4.
5.	5.
6.	6.

Blending Expertise to Create Partnership

With your co-teaching partner, compare notes on the knowledge, skills, and characteristics you bring to a co-teaching partnership. Complete a Venn diagram like the one below and then respond to the questions that follow.

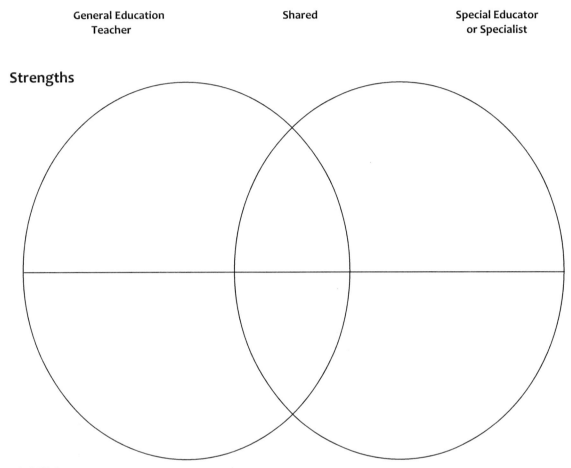

General Education Teacher   Shared   Special Educator or Specialist

Strengths

Liabilities

1. In what ways are you and your teaching partner similar? How might your similarities contribute to the effectiveness of your co-teaching? How might they detract from it?

2. In what ways are you and your teaching partner different? How might your differences contribute to the effectiveness of your co-teaching? How might they detract from it?

3. As you review what each of you bring to your partnership, what are areas that neither of you mentioned that might enhance your instruction? How could you work together to be sure that you incorporate such areas into your shared teaching (e.g., strategies for increasing student engagement)?

Chapter 4
Co-Teaching Approaches

Quality is never an accident; it is always the result of high intention,
sincere effort, intelligent direction and skillful execution;
it represents the wise choice of many alternatives.

~William Foster

Learner Objectives

1. Describe six approaches for structuring co-taught classrooms, including examples, opportunities, challenges, and variations for each one.

2. List factors that may influence which co-teaching approaches you select.

3. Generate ideas to make the best instructional use of two professionals in the classroom for students with diverse needs.

Although successful co-teaching relies on many factors, perhaps the most essential dimension is the effective arrangement of the teachers and students so that learning is maximized. That is the focus of this chapter.

As you think about what a two-teacher classroom is like, keep in mind these points. First co-teaching should be deliberate, that is, it should be designed based on an understanding of the content to be covered and the needs of students in the classroom (for example, Friend, Cook, Hurley-Chamberlain, & Shamberger, 2010; Gurgur & Uzuner, 2011; Sileo & van Garderen, 2010). Although all co-teachers occasionally have days in which one person runs into the classroom saying "What are we doing today?," if this is the typical practice, it is unlikely the potential of co-teaching can be reached.

Second, part of the reason that co-teaching must be deliberate is because it is how students with disabilities receive the specialized instruction outlined on their individualized education programs (IEPs) and ELLs receive instruction based on their individual learning plans (ILPs). Part of co-teaching must include opportunities for students to work on reaching their IEP goals, English learning goals, speech/language goals, or reading goals, depending on student need, but that should occur, as much as possible, within the context of the overall instructional program. In fact, if specialized instruction is not part of co-teaching, a valid question might be raised about the purpose for having two professionals in a single class. This topic is addressed in detail in Chapter 5.

Third, co-teaching presumes flexibility in terms of roles and responsibilities in the classroom. That is, sometimes the general educator is working with the large group and sometimes it is the special educator or other specialist with that group. Sometimes both teachers are working with small groups. Remediation is not the sole responsibility of the specialist, and both teachers work with all the students in the class. They also share tasks such as discipline and classroom management.

Finally, co-teaching should always have the impact of *increasing instructional intensity* (III). That is, as teachers consider the approaches and make decisions about which to use and how to group students, they should constantly analyze whether their practices actively engage both professionals in teaching, improve the quality of instruction for their diverse learners, and result in improved student outcomes.

Six Co-Teaching Approaches

Co-teaching can be accomplished by arranging teachers and students using six specific approaches (Friend & Cook, 2013). These approaches are illustrated in Figures 4.1-4.6 as each is explained. Each one has advantages and drawbacks, and no single approach is considered to be the best one. You should think of these six approaches as a beginning since they do not at all represent the many variations creative co-teachers have invented in order to meet students' needs. Similarly, you should not think of the approaches as existing in isolation. You might find that you use two or more approaches during a single lesson or that you blend the approaches to create new options. Finally, the goal is not to choose just one of these approaches. Generally, you and your teaching partner should implement at least three approaches even when you have just begun to co-teach, and you eventually should employ all of them to create the best learning opportunities for the students for whom they are responsible. As you explore the co-teaching approaches, refer to the planning form included in this chapter's appendix. Use a lesson that you'll teach soon, and design alternative ways to present it using one or more of the approaches.

One teaching, one observing

Recommended Use: Frequent, but usually for relatively brief periods of time

Decision-making in today's schools should be made based on data. Co-teaching gives educators a unique opportunity to gather important data that then can be used to improve student learning. In one teaching, one observing, one teacher manages the instruction of the entire student group while the other teacher systematically gathers data the two educators have decided are important. With the current heightened emphasis on student performance and data-driven instructional decision-making, this approach generally should be used at least several times each week, even daily, so that instruction can be appropriately designed and adapted to respond to student needs. However, the observation of students also should be used periodically as a concern arises (for example, several students are displaying increasingly disruptive behavior during class) or as teachers identify a specific type of information they need to monitor student progress (for example, assessment of an English language learner's vocabulary use during class discussion). Overall, data collection may focus on one student, a small group of targeted or representative students, or the entire class.

Many strategies are available to gather data in a co-taught classroom, and special educators, at least, usually have had one or more university courses that directly address this topic. For example, they probably have learned how to complete an *ABC analysis,* which stands for antecedents-behaviors-consequences. This technique is helpful when teachers are trying to determine what is causing a particular behavior to occur. Another data collection strategy is *event recording,* where each time a behavior occurs it is noted. This strategy might be used to count how many times a student leaves his seat or calls out. Yet another observation technique is *interval recording.* In interval recording, a period of time is divided into brief segments (for example, 15 minutes divided into 15 or 30 segments). The teacher observing simply marks whether the behavior under observation occurs during each of the segments. This technique might be used when the teachers suspect a student is frequently calling out during large-group instruction. Yet another strategy is *duration recording,* in which one teacher records how long a behavior occurs. This might be used to measure how long it takes certain students to begin assigned work or for how long some students work before they become distracted.

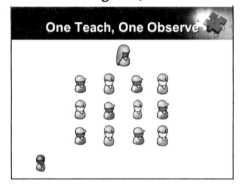

Figure 4.1

One Teach, One Observe

These data collection ideas are just a few of the many that special educators and other specialists have learned. These professionals also recognize that the specific approach to gathering observational data is determined by the goal for doing so, and they can help ensure that observing students results in valuable information that can be used to make classroom decisions.

One last point should be made about the observation of students as part of co-teaching: Data collection has been simplified greatly over the past few years with the growing use of tablet devices and smartphones. Today, many co-teachers are using electronic spreadsheets or various apps to gather data, thus making it easier to accumulate important student information, share it, and make decisions on the basis of the data.

One teaching, one observing in practice. Here are three examples of co-teachers using one teaching, one observing. Which recording strategy did the teachers use? How do you think they might change their instruction or classroom procedures based on the data they obtained?

- Two teachers are thinking that the school's intervention team should discuss a student struggling to learn. They decide to observe the student working individually in order to gain insight on what he does when he cannot answer a specific question, how long he works before becoming distracted, and who he asks for assistance from among his classmates.

- In a high school classroom, the teachers would like to know which students attempt to answer teacher questions during large group instruction. Using a seating chart, one teacher tallies which students raise their hands as questions are asked.

- In a middle school math class, students work on individual whiteboards, solving problems related to order of operations. One teacher walks through the classroom as the students work, recording — before students wipe their whiteboards clean — which students solved each problem correctly.

- In any co-taught classroom, the teachers have created a spreadsheet that summarizes across columns the standards to be addressed for that 9-week period. Student names are listed in the first column, and as questions are asked or activities are completed through which the standards are being assessed, one of the teachers checks off which students demonstrate mastery.

Opportunities and challenges. Two teachers have the chance to focus on students in a way that one teacher would never have the time to do, and so this co-teaching approach enables teachers to know subtleties about their students' learning needs. In some cases, though, teachers may wish to discuss what types of data would be helpful to have, how the data could be gathered, and how the data would be interpreted and used for instruction. Unfortunately, in professional development sessions, teachers — from elementary, middle school, and high school — often comment that they have never collected observational data on their students. For them, conversations are needed about the imperatives of having data to make instructional decisions and realistic ways to gather and use it. Another point of conversation might include deciding who should observe, including why it is important for both teachers to have opportunities to step back to formally gather data about student learning and behavior.

Variations on the approach. All of the examples provided thus far have focused on gathering data on students' academic, behavior, and social skills. A key variation of this approach shifts to looking at teachers' behaviors. Before describing this option, though, a caution is in order. Teachers in new partnerships probably should wait until they are comfortable with each other and their classroom practices before using this variation. Further, in situations where tension exists between co-teachers, this variation is probably not a good idea to use because it might be viewed as evaluative of the teacher leading instruction. All of that said, one teaching, one observing can be a valuable way for teachers to monitor their own skills — outside a formal evaluation or mentoring process. For example, in addition to tallying which students raised their hands in the example presented earlier, teachers may decide to assess whether they call on boys and girls proportionately. They also may wish to know whether they are asking students various levels of questions and not just questions that tap basic comprehension. Another example concerns consistency in responding to student misbehavior. Does each teacher react in the same way, or does one have a stronger reaction than the other? With the rapidly spreading use of a new generation of teacher evaluation systems, co-teachers have the opportunity to help each other meet the expectations of such systems through reciprocal observations; thus, they may be better prepared when an administrator completes the formal observation process. What other teacher behaviors could you and a co-teacher decide to observe? How might data on those behaviors influence your co-teaching?

Station Teaching

Recommended Use: Frequent

In any material you read that discusses the topic of meeting the needs of diverse groups of learners, an always-recommended strategy is grouping students in various ways in order to better tailor instruction. This makes sense. Small groups can be arranged by skill level or by student interest. They can be based on mixing students at various learning levels or with different styles of social interaction.

When co-teaching is in place, the options for using small groups become even greater.

In the basic station teaching approach, teachers divide the content to be addressed into three segments and then group students so that one-third begins with each part of the content. Each teacher works with a group, and the third group works independently. During the lesson, the student groups rotate from station to station so that, by its conclusion, all the students have completed all three, and the teachers have each worked with every student in the class.

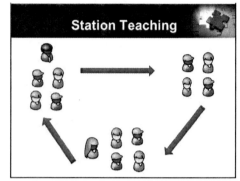

Figure 4.2

Elementary teachers may be familiar with the similar concept of centers; the difference with stations is that two of the groups are teacher facilitated while in centers teachers usually monitor all the groups' activities. This approach is not as common in middle and high schools, but teachers there also are recognizing the value of this instructional grouping option, especially if they are in a block-scheduling arrangement.

Station teaching in practice. Here are examples of co-teaching using stations:

🧩 In an elementary math class, students are learning about estimating. One group of students is estimating distance (for example, estimating how many footsteps it would take to walk around the perimeter of the classroom), one group is estimating time (for example, how many times you can jump up and down in one minute), and one group is estimating mass (for example, how many crayons will it take to balance the weights already on the balance scale). The first two groups are led by teachers; the third is independently completed by students working with a partner. During this 45-minute instructional period, all students rotate to all three stations.

🧩 In a high school U.S. history class (in a block schedule), students are studying the industrial revolution. One group of students, led by a teacher, is discussing *The Jungle* by Upton Sinclair. A second group is reviewing material from the textbook with the other teacher. The third group is examining materials provided by the local historical society, including old photos depicting life at the beginning of the twentieth century. The students are discussing what life was like then and writing fictionalized life stories about the individuals portrayed in the photos.

🧩 In a middle school English class, teachers have designed instruction based on principles of the Common Core State Standards. In one group, students are led by a teacher to work on close reading, looking for repeated phrases in the literature being read and analyzing why that technique is effective. A second group is working with the other teacher on the academic vocabulary related to this current unit of instruction. In the third group, students are addressing stamina, that is, they have an extended reading assignment that they are completing independently.

Opportunities and challenges. Station teaching has many advantages. For example, by grouping students in various ways, teachers can more effectively reach instructional goals. For some activities, groups should be heterogeneous; for others, they could be skill-based. Station teaching also enables teachers to keep very close watch on student learning; with just eight or ten students in a group, it is much easier than in the large group to see which students have understood the lesson and which need additional support. This co-teaching approach also lets teachers divide students who have behavior problems or difficulty working with each other. Finally, station teaching facilitates a highly interactive instructional environment. With multiple groups and multiple teachers, lessons can incorporate more student participation through discussion and activities.

However, station teaching also comes with some cautions. First, the activities that occur at each station must function independently of each other. If students must complete one station in order to do the next, this approach is not the one to use. For example, if teachers want students to pre-write, then draft an essay, and then edit the essay with their peers, station teaching is not appropriate — it would require that some students be assigned to edit before writing! If you review all the examples given, you'll see that each one meets this criterion. Each station can be successfully completed whether it is first, second, or third in the student's rotation.

Other cautions about station teaching concern logistics. Noise level can rise when small groups are used, and co-teachers may need to discuss how to keep everyone engaged but the noise level acceptable to both teachers and students. In addition, this co-teaching approach requires attention to timing. A planning task is to be sure the instruction and activities for each station require approximately the same amount of time. During the lesson, some co-teachers use an Internet-based timer that displays for both teachers and students the time remaining for the station.

Variations on the approach. The primary variations of station teaching concern changing the number of groups to suit the co-teaching situation. For example, in a middle or high school with traditional as opposed to block schedules or in an elementary school when student behavior is a major concern, three stations in a class period may not be feasible or realistic. In that case, the teachers might plan just two stations, eliminating the independent station. Further, the teachers could decide that when it is time to change stations, the teachers will move instead of the students, thus saving valuable instructional time and possibly avoiding student behavior challenges during a transition. Another option for secondary educators in traditionally-scheduled schools is to use station teaching as part of a two-day lesson plan. During the first part of the first day, the teachers might team. During the second half of that period, students complete the first of three stations. When they return the next day, they complete the two remaining stations. In high schools, teacher occasionally extend this thinking further by planning a three-day lesson in which students remain in a single station for an entire class period.

Other options related to the number of groups also exist. For example, sometimes in elementary grades, additional adults are available (for example, a paraprofessional or parent volunteer) and so teachers may increase the number of stations, holding core instruction themselves but having the other adults lead review or practice stations. In secondary settings, teachers sometimes establish four, five, or even six stations, having students work independently in smaller groups, for example, working various types of math problems interspersed with stations led by the two teachers.

Parallel Teaching

Recommended Use: Frequent

Are you the type of person who is most comfortable when you can blend in with a large group? Are you uncomfortable when you are called upon to answer a question or when everyone turns to listen to your opinion? As an adult, your preference is just that — a preference. However, some students feel this same way — and if they do not call attention to themselves they sometimes cruise through their education, perhaps not achieving in the way they would if they received more individualized attention. Parallel teaching permits teachers to provide that attention.

In the basic version of parallel teaching, professionals divide students into two groups and lead the same instruction with both of them. That is, they may both address the math objective for the day by introducing students to regrouping with zeroes, finding the volume of a prism, or conducting a review session for the unit exam to be given the next day. In this co-

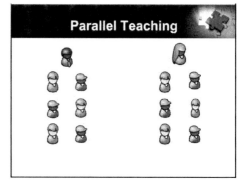

Figure 4.3

Parallel Teaching

teaching approach, students receive instruction from one of the teachers, but not both; the groups do not rotate.

Parallel teaching in practice. Here are examples of parallel teaching as implemented by experienced co-teachers.

- In a sixth grade English/language arts class the students are reading *Bridge to Terabithia* by Katherine Paterson. They have read the first four chapters, and it is time for discussion to check comprehension, analyze character traits, and consider the themes of the novel. The teachers divide the students into two heterogeneous groups, paying attention to which students tend to have lots to say during discussions and which tend to be quiet. Once divided, each teacher discusses with students Jess and Leslie's friendship, using these questions:

    ♦ Do you think Jess and Leslie's friendship is believable? Why or why not? What evidence from the text supports your view?

    ♦ Have you ever been friends with someone who is different than you? How were you different? Did this make your friendship easier or harder? Why?

    ♦ How do you think Jess and Leslie's friendship will influence what else occurs in this novel? What is your justification for your answer?

    By having the discussions running concurrently, each student has the opportunity to discuss their own experiences with friendships and seek clues from the literature that support or refute their views, and the teachers can ensure that even students usually reluctant to participate can do so.

- The objectives for students in a chemistry class are to

    ♦ Distinguish between chemical reactions that are reversible and those that go to completion.

    ♦ Explain the concept of chemical equilibrium

    ♦ Understand how Le Chatelier's Principle works on a chemical reaction at equilibrium.

    In a large group, the students have observed and participated in several demonstrations of reversible chemical reactions (for example, hot wheels cars that change color with temperature), those that go to completion (for example, burning a match), and chemical equilibrium (for example, NO_2-N_2O_4 gas tubes in both cold and hot water). The teachers then divide the students into two groups to discuss what they have observed and to generate examples from everyday life that demonstrate chemical equilibrium. Each group produces a chart of their responses, and they are posted so everyone in class can see them; homework for students is to design a controlled paper wad fight that would demonstrate the principle of equilibrium.

🧩 In an elementary class, the standard being addressed is main idea and supporting details. The teacher divides the class in half so that as the students read several short passages, each student has twice as many opportunities to participate in the discussion of identifying these key components of paragraphs.

Opportunities and challenges. The opportunities and challenges of parallel teaching are very similar to those of station teaching. That is, this co-teaching approach permits teachers to assign students to groups to maximize student participation and minimize behavior problems. It increases the number of times that each student can respond during teacher-led instruction, and it increases instructional intensity by ensuring that each teacher has an active role in the classroom.

Potential challenges in parallel teaching include these: First, this approach is only effective if the teachers can offer equivalent instruction to students. If one teacher is unsure of the material being taught, the students she works with would be at a disadvantage during a learning assessment. This often implies that if the special educator, ESL teacher, or other specialist is not highly qualified in the content area in which co-teaching is occurring, parallel teaching is reserved mostly as a technique for review or discussion after initial core academic instruction has occurred.

Second, this approach requires that teachers take about the same amount of time to complete instruction, and teachers have to learn to pace their lessons accordingly. Third, noise level can be significant during parallel teaching, and teachers may need to discuss their tolerance for noise as well as that of students.

Variations on the approach. Parallel teaching is a flexible means for enhancing instruction. For example, two additional types of parallel teaching are often implemented. First, when students are at two different skill levels, teachers may group students based on those learning levels. They would put the several struggling students in one group, the highest achievers in the other group, and heterogeneously assign the other students so as to avoid negative bias. For example, in a math class the teachers together discussed and demonstrated multiplication. After the lesson, the students were divided into two groups based on their level of understanding. One group worked on multiplication problems using manipulatives while the other did the same problems without manipulatives. Other examples of using deliberate grouping in parallel teaching include grouping students based on interest (e.g., one group reads a short story with a sports theme while the other group reads a short story with a music theme) or projects (for example, based on the same unit, one group prepares multimedia slides and presents to the class while the other group writes a skit about the topic and presents it).

Second, parallel teaching sometimes is used to present different points of view on a single topic. Two teachers introduce the causes of the Civil War by having one group learn about the perspectives of the states that seceded from the Union, emphasizing their perception of the "War of Northern Aggression." The other group learns about the issues of slavery and human rights. After the two groups complete their lesson, they join for a whole-class debate. Notice how this application of parallel teaching could be used in any instruction where the goal was to help students understand multiple points of view (for example, characters' perspectives, a piece of literature taught in English or language arts, different ways to solve equations, scientific debates).

Alternative Teaching

Recommended Use: Occasional

Co-teachers often understand their students' needs in a way that one teacher cannot. They may find that some students have quickly mastered certain concepts and might benefit from enrichment, or they may note that some students struggling with the content would benefit from additional direct instruction. Similarly, they may realize that several students share a particular interest or that a few students are better able to focus when they work in a small group led by one of the teachers.

Figure 4.4

All of the implied instructional needs in these examples could easily be met using alternative teaching. In this approach, one teacher manages the large group while the other takes a small group for a specific instructional purpose. This small group might meet for a few minutes while other students check homework or complete a warm-up task, or it might meet after initial instruction occurs. In elementary schools, the small group could meet either later or earlier in the day, or possibly during a transition immediately prior to the initial core instruction.

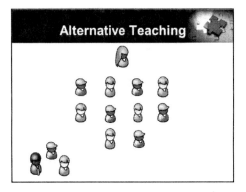

Alternative teaching in practice. These examples of alternative teaching are designed to demonstrate the wide variety of instructional needs it can address:

🏫 Two elementary teachers know they have several students who would benefit from pre-teaching. Before they begin the unit on land formations, they decide to pull a group to introduce the new vocabulary. Among the students in the group are Simon, a student with a significant learning disability in the area of reading; Mitchell, a student who takes medication for ADHD; Charity, a student who is uncertain of herself and tends to avoid participation in a group unless she is sure she knows the answer; and Maria, an English language learner who struggles with her schoolwork. The general education teacher completes a mini-lesson on the vocabulary (for example, plain, mesa, isthmus, peninsula) while the special education teacher finishes helping students put away materials from their writing project and prepare for social studies.

♦ In 7th grade math, the co-teachers have completed a two-day lesson that addresses these objectives:

- ♦ Identify and apply properties of real numbers, including pi.
- ♦ Select and apply instruments (including rulers) and units of measure to the degree of accuracy required.
- ♦ Use concrete and graphic representations and applicable formulae to find the perimeter of two-dimensional figures.

The students have measured several round objects in the room (for example, the base of a coffee can) to determine perimeter and circumference. They then divide the circumference by the diameter and learn that this number approximates pi. During the second day, while some students independently complete a worksheet extending this concept, the general education teacher works with six students who do not yet seem to understand the concept. They measure additional objects, complete the division, and compare their answers to pi.

♦ The students in the 9th grade co-teaching section are being assessed on academic vocabulary considered prerequisite for entry to high school. Across a three-day period, students move to a small group for this assessment. The teachers use these data to determine which students will need extensive assistance related to academic vocabulary and which exceed expectations and so will need extension or enrichment.

Opportunities and challenges. Many co-teachers worry that students with disabilities or those who are English language learners may not receive the individual attention they need in a large class group. Alternative teaching permits teachers to conduct those intense, small-group sessions within the context of the classroom. This co-teaching approach also can provide instructional flexibility. That is, teachers may use it to provide enrichment, remediation, assessment or pre-teaching. Alternative teaching also can enable teachers to have more personalized interactions with students.

The most obvious challenge to this co-teaching approach is preventing the small group from being seen as the equivalent of a pullout special class in the corner of the room. If students perceive that classmates with special needs are repeatedly identified to participate in the small group, the core co-teaching concept of seamless education without stigma is violated.

To avoid this problem, co-teachers can use several strategies. First, they can vary who is leading instruction for the small group. If the general education teacher sometimes works with the group needing remediation, less stigma may occur. Second, the teachers can clearly vary the purposes of the group, making sure they use alternative teaching for at least three different instructional purposes. Finally, using a class roster and a form like the one included in the appendix at the end of this chapter, co-teachers can keep a record of which students have been placed into the small group so they can track to be sure all students occasionally work in the small group, and no student is in the small group every time this approach is employed.

Variations on the approach. The examples provided thus far were set in the context of academic instruction. However, alternative teaching can be effective for managing student behavior as well. For example, if one or two students tend to be disruptive and, despite teachers' best efforts, are interfering with the progress of classmates, the co-teachers might decide to spend a couple of days with those two students in a small group that also includes two positive role models and a student who just transferred to the district. The teacher working with the small group follows the same lesson plan as the teacher leading the large group. By placing the students with behavior concerns in a small group supervised by one teacher and incorporating instruction on appropriate interactions with peers, their learning can be focused and the rest of the class can progress as well.

Teaming

Recommended Use: Occasional

Some teachers describe co-teaching as having "one brain in two bodies." They refer to finishing each other's sentences and to the wonderful choreography of a two-teacher classroom. These teachers generally are discussing teaming.

In teaming, both teachers are in front of the classroom, sharing the responsibility of leading instruction, as when the kindergarten co-teachers together instruct children about their community or middle school English teachers begin teaching students about rhythm and rhyme. Alternatively, co-teachers may have different but equally active roles, as when one teacher leads a large-group lesson while the other teacher models note-taking on the Smartboard™ or one teacher states directions while the other demonstrates them. The key characteristic of this co-teaching approach is that both teachers are fully engaged in the delivery of the core academic instruction.

Teaming in practice. Co-teachers use teaming at all grade levels and across all subject areas. Here are three examples:

🧩 In algebra, co-teachers are working with students on the concepts of lines and slopes. The day's lesson includes writing an equation for a line already known. After reviewing how to graph a line, how to determine slope, and how to determine whether lines intercept, the students are being introduced to writing an equation for a line already known. At the beginning of this lesson, the specialist leads during the review and the general education teacher demonstrates the concepts using graphs that have been loaded for use on the Smartboard™, interjecting clarifying questions. When the new concept is introduced, the general education teacher takes more of a lead while the specialist moves to the board, working examples and interjecting questions as the general education teacher had done during the first part of the lesson.

🧩 In a second grade classroom, the teachers have used the book *How Big is a Foot?* by Rolf Myller as part of a unit on linear measure. In the story, the bed ordered for the queen's birthday ends up being too short because the order was placed based on the length of the king's long feet, but it was made by the craftsman whose feet were much shorter. The point for students is that measures are consistent so that results are reliable. The teachers come to class the day of the lesson wearing different shoes: One has on brightly colored shoes, but they are just her typical size. The other has on a pair of her son's size 17 sneakers. The teachers demonstrate the difference in "six feet" when shoe size is the measure and introduce the ruler, comparing it to each of the shoes. After the teachers encourage the students to estimate how many non-standard and standard feet are in several examples of taped lines they have put on the floor of the classroom, the students all trace their own shoes, cut out the outlines, compare them to a standard foot (the ruler), measure several additional items, and then write a paragraph about their learning.

Figure 4.5

🧩 In a middle school science class, the teachers are debating whether global warming is something created by people or a natural phenomenon. Each makes several points. The students then are divided into groups (parallel teaching) to conduct further research on each point of view and later will continue the debate themselves.

Opportunities and challenges. Teaming can be very energizing. Some teachers comment that when working with a partner they are willing to try new ways to reach students they never would have tried if teaching alone. They also increase the entertainment/engagement factor of teaching: Through instructional conversations, sharing question-asking, and the antics that sometimes are part of this co-teaching approach, students are more likely to remain attentive.

As with all co-teaching approaches, however, this one also has some challenges. You may have been surprised that this approach is recommended for occasional rather than frequent use. That is because this approach loses the valuable instructional technique of grouping. When both teachers are in front of the class, they may not be as aware of the individual and subtle needs of their students. Further, with two teachers delivering whole-group instruction, students may have too few opportunities to respond.

A second challenge of teaming relates to the teachers' professional relationship. If you and your co-teacher have just begun your partnership or are not very comfortable working together in the classroom, this approach may call for more flexibility than can reasonably be expected. That is, some co-teachers may use this approach intuitively and almost as soon as they begin co-teaching, some may use it once they learn each other's styles and develop instructional trust, and some may find teaming just is not an approach they can easily implement.

Finally, if both partners tend to talk quite a bit, teaming may have an additional challenge. One teacher may provide an example, which prompts the other teacher to give another example, and so on. Co-teachers may have to gauge their contributions so that pacing is maintained, staying aware that their own interaction patterns during teaching may slow lessons down.

Variations on the approach. Teaming can bring out the creative side of teachers. When elementary teaching partners were introducing the concepts of vertical and horizontal, one teacher wore a blouse with vertical stripes while the other wore a shirt with horizontal stripes. They each explained the concept their clothing was illustrating. Two high school teachers in an English class acted out scenes from *Of Mice and Men* to help students grasp key events and themes. In a middle school science class, one teacher usually gives directions for the lab while the other demonstrates the directions, quizzing students, occasionally making intentional mistakes to check student comprehension, and asking the students to repeat directions to confirm understanding.

Overall, teaming is an option for partners to bring to the instructional situation what each has as a first area of expertise, as discussed in Chapter 1 — core academic content for the general education teachers and learning process for the special education and ESL teachers.

One Teaching, One Assisting

Recommended Use: Seldom (or less)

The final co-teaching approach places one teacher in a lead role while the other clearly is functioning as a support to the classroom. In this approach, one teacher leads the instruction while the other monitors student work, addresses behavior issues, answers student questions, and facilitates instruction by distributing papers or other materials. The teacher who is assisting might sometimes ask the leading teacher a question to clarify a concept or direction he has noticed is a problem for the students. In some settings, one teaching, one assisting frequently serves as a type of informal observation.

One teaching, one assisting in practice. One teaching, one assisting can be helpful in certain types of instructional situations. Here are two examples:

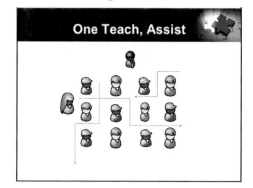

Figure 4.6

One Teach, Assist

- In biology, students are learning about chromatography as a means to separate mixtures. Objectives include these:

  - Perform a paper chromatography separation of pigment mixture and analyze its separate parts by determining the R_f (retention factor).
  - Using leaf chromatography, show that the R_f is a constant.

  The students have experimented using grape Kool-Aid and water-based markers. As they begin to use crushed fresh leaves in a solution, a procedure that calls for patience on the part of students and careful attention to detail. As the filter paper is dipped into the leaf and solvent mixture, one teacher continues to provide instruction and directions while the other moves around the classroom, checking to be sure each student is completing the experiment correctly.

- The fifth grade class is reviewing long division. One teacher writes a problem on the board, and the students all solve it using individual whiteboards and markers. At the other teacher's signal, they all hold up their whiteboards, and the assisting teacher scans to be sure that all the students have completed the problem correctly.

Opportunities and challenges. The opportunities related to one teaching, one assisting generally relate to the provision of individual and classroom support. An example of individual support comes from high schools, where some students have noted that they like having the option of quietly signaling the assisting teacher to have a quick question answered or word defined. It is less embarrassing than raising their hands and asking their questions in front of the whole class. Classroom support has already been illustrated: By having one teacher check student responses and carry out management tasks such as distributing materials, instruction can be effective and efficient.

Of all the co-teaching approaches, however, one teaching, one assisting has the greatest potential to be over-used and abused. In fact, this approach to co-teaching is the one that co-teaching supervisors and observers worry about the most. In too many classrooms, the general education teacher continues to teach as she did in a one-teacher class while the special educator or ESL teacher works either as a passive partner who waits for instruction to finish before helping students who struggle to learn or as a highly paid teaching assistant. Even if the teachers reverse roles occasionally (although when this approach is used too frequently, that generally is not the case), the problem is not diminished. The classroom still has just one teacher, thus eliminating the entire wealth of instructional possibilities that would otherwise be possible.

Some teachers indicate that they use this approach to help students attend to instruction. However, when a teacher stops to talk to a student, it is a likely that he will completely shift the student's attention rather than focusing it, and the student may miss a key concept being explained by the other teacher. Other teachers say this is their primary approach because the specialist is not familiar with the core curriculum. If that is the case, the teachers should discuss other options for co-teaching so that partnership can grow. Yet other teachers use this approach because they lack planning time. That topic is addressed in Chapter 6, but it is not an excuse for over-using one teaching, one assisting.

Perhaps of most concern is that this approach encourages students to become dependent on teacher support rather than fostering independence in learning. When a teacher is always available, some students will, without fail, ask for help. Ultimately, comments made to specialists by students in classrooms where this approach is too common illustrate its dangers:

- *Do they pay you to do this?*
- *Are they ever going to let you have your own classroom?*
- *I don't have to listen to you. You're not the real teacher.*

Variations on the approach. So many cautions should be kept in mind about one teaching, one assisting that mentioning variations on the approach seems to raise the likelihood that it will be used inappropriately, and so perhaps one additional point of emphasis should be made instead. If this approach is used, both teachers should have opportunities to take on both roles, and they should deliberately ensure that they both work with all the students in the class so that no stigma results from any student-teacher interaction.

Selecting Co-Teaching Approaches

The six co-teaching approaches provide a framework for thinking about what a co-taught class should be like. However, co-teachers may find that they use certain approaches more than others and that they have questions about implementing them.

Factors That May Influence Co-Teaching

Several suggestions can be given regarding selecting co-teaching approaches. How does each of these areas affect your thinking about using the co-teaching approaches?

Student characteristics and needs. As you might guess, students are the first consideration in selecting co-teaching approaches. For example, if your students easily handle transitions between activities and generally are focused on instruction, you probably can use any of the approaches that have been described. However, if your students are easily distracted or tend to become disruptive during transitions, you might choose approaches with less student movement such as parallel teaching or teaming. Here are other examples of student characteristics that might affect your selection of approaches — and you probably can think of others:

- Specific instructional needs of individual students
- Student need for structure and predictability
- Student attentional skills
- Diversity of student learning levels represented in the class
- Physical or sensory needs of students (for example, need for an interpreter, need for wheelchair access to all parts of the room), and
- Student use of assistive technology (for example, need for a communication board or computer/tablet device access).

Teacher characteristics and preferences. You and your teaching partner represent a second factor that affects the selection of approaches. For example, if you and your co-teacher are just beginning your partership, you might begin with mostly parallel or station teaching with just a little use of one teaching and one assisting (both teachers taking on both roles, of course). This combination of approaches establishes clearly that two teachers are present in the classroom, avoids the risk of re-creating a pullout remedial program that could occur with alternative teaching, and provides immediate benefit to students, who experience increased instructional intensity (III). Two teachers who have co-taught before might make different selections based on their experiences.

Sometimes one teacher is more comfortable with the idea of two-teacher classroom than the other, regardless of their co-teaching history. In these situations, the teachers might decide that the first four weeks of the partnership will be spent primarily in observing and assisting while their relationship develops, but they then should move beyond the beginner stage. A similar approach to developing effective classroom practices might also be needed if the special educator or ESL teacher in a middle or high school does not have the content academic knowledge necessary to take a lead role in the class. For example, Jamie, a special educator who co-teaches geometry with Chris, a math teacher with 12 years of experience, may feel intimidated. Jamie may not have studied geometry since her own high school days, and she may fear making mistakes and causing Chris to have to take over to correct her. The same gradual approach of building a classroom partnership is in order. What is not acceptable is for Chris to decide that for the entire first year Jamie should mostly assist in order to learn the curriculum. While the second co-teaching year for these professionals undoubtedly will be richer and more comfortable than the first, they should actively work to gradually increase Jamie's participation throughout the first year. Said directly, professionals are not entitled to a year's salary for merely learning the middle school or high school curriculum in which they are co-teaching.

One other factor for teachers to keep in mind as they co-teach is relative to the experience of the teachers and the effect it may have on structuring co-taught lessons. Think about these combinations, introduced in Chapter 3: two novice or early career teachers, two veteran teachers, one novice teacher and one experienced teacher. What strengths might each of these combinations of professionals have? What concerns might result just because of their experience levels?

Features of the curriculum. Although creative teachers are constantly finding ways to use all the co-teaching approaches at all levels and across all academic subject matter, teachers might find, especially at the beginning, that their subject matter makes certain approaches more attractive than others. For example, in elementary reading programs in which students are grouped by their skill levels, station teaching is likely to be frequently used. In middle school math, teachers may find that they can ensure student understanding and check students' work for accuracy most efficiently by using parallel teaching. In a high school civics and government class, though, the teachers may find that teaming is appropriate when combined with alternative teaching for work on special projects. The point of thinking about curriculum is this: When co-teaching is a new endeavor, use structures that most easily match the curriculum. As the partnership grows, try to expand the number of approaches used in order to achieve increased instructional intensity.

Logistics issues. Two concerns about using the co-teaching approaches often arise: time for planning and space limitations resulting from crowded classrooms. Finding time for shared planning is addressed in detail in Chapter 6. Here, a specific bit of advice can be offered. If teachers have limited or non-existent planning time, they should consider basing their co-teaching on the patterns that occur in instruction. If certain lessons tend to involve introducing a lot of vocabulary, the teachers might use station teaching whenever those lessons occur. When a unit is being reviewed, they might decide generally to select parallel teaching. During the weekly review on Fridays, alternative teaching may be the approach of choice. That is, when planning time is limited, finding efficient ways to structure the classroom can make effective co-teaching more feasible.

Space sometimes is a serious concern for co-teachers. A spacious classroom does make using the six approaches more feasible, but even in a crowded classroom you should experiment with several student grouping strategies. For example, in parallel, station, or alternative teaching, you might have the teachers move to work with different student groups instead of having the students move. In elementary and middle schools, you also could have one group of students seated closely together on the floor while the other group works at desks. Another option is to use all the approaches but to be sure that classroom furniture is arranged to accommodate them before the lesson begins. Using two spaces (for example, expanding to use the empty classroom across the hall) sometimes is appropriate, but care must be taken that co-teaching does not become simply a questionable means of reducing class size. In addition, legal issues could arise if students with disabilities are often instructed in a separate location when their IEPs indicated a general education setting. Similarly, problems may occur in terms of the core academic subject highly-qualified status of the specialist.

Additional Considerations

In observing co-teachers and interacting with them in all types of schools in all parts of the country, several other topics are mentioned often enough that they should be noted here.

Non-approaches. A few teachers somehow arrive at the decision that co-teaching means they take turns. One way they decide to take turns is to alternate weeks (or units or chapters) in terms or planning and leading instruction. Dividing teaching in this way undermines the entire point of co-teaching — it doesn't draw on the strengths that each professional brings to the situation. Another example of taking turns may occur even if the teachers jointly plan instruction. They may say, "I lead on Mondays and he leads on Tuesdays. That way we're sure we both teach." Comments such as these usually suggest that the teachers have not embraced the collaborative dimension of co-teaching and are at a very early stage in the development of their practice. In both types of turn-taking, the fundamental issue becomes one of the value of having two teachers in the classroom. If turns are taken, the situation looks remarkably like job sharing instead of co-teaching.

Tailoring approaches to your situation. As you experiment with the co-teaching approaches, you'll probably discover that you sometimes blend two or more approaches in a single lesson, create your own variations of them, and develop your own signature co-teaching structures. An example occurs when teachers blend parallel teaching and station teaching, splitting students into two groups and then again splitting those groups again for conferencing or instruction with half of each. As you think of innovative options, you should congratulate yourselves — this means your understanding of co-teaching and its power is maturing and becoming integral to instruction. The six approaches truly are intended to be just a starting point, a way of discussing co-teaching that permits clear explanations and options for painting verbal pictures of co-taught classrooms. They are the basis for moving to a new level that can be uniquely yours.

Rethinking common teacher practices. Some professionals may find that co-teaching causes them to rethink some of the habits they have developed as effective teachers, a topic introduced in Chapter 3. For example, when working with a small group of students, most teachers sit so that they face the classroom in order to ensure that other students are working. In co-teaching, however, when two teachers are simultaneously working with student groups, they may find it is better to position themselves parallel to each other (that is, both with their backs to the same wall) or back-to-back (that is, toward the center of the classroom so their voices are directed to opposite walls). The latter two options help the teachers from talking over each other and distracting students. When you teach, do you often use choral responding to increase student participation? That's a great idea and can be effective in co-taught classes during teaming or other large group activities. However, when students are in small groups it can be distracting. An alternative is to have available for each student a personal white board or slate on which answers can be written and then displayed. What other nonverbal strategies could you use during co-teaching to address noise level while keeping students actively participating? Are there other teaching habits you have or your partner has that could affect your use of the co-teaching approaches?

For Further Thought

1. As you think about the co-teaching in which you participate or are planning, which approaches seem most suited to your situation? Why? What does your co-teacher think?

2. Which approach have you used least in your co-teaching? How could you use this approach (either alone or blended with others) in an upcoming lesson?

3. What factors may influence your decisions about co-teaching approaches? Why? How do your perceptions compare with those of your co-teacher? How might the developmental status of your professional relationship influence how you arrange the teachers and students in the class?

4. How can you avoid or reduce the problem of too much use of one teaching, one assisting? What plans could you and your co-teacher make to address this topic?

Taking Action

1. Conduct an anonymous survey of all the co-teaching partners in your school using the form included in the appendix for this chapter. What do the results tell you about use of the co-teaching approaches in your school? Have a co-teaching brainstorming session to generate new ideas for expanding the use of the co-teaching approaches that can have the greatest positive impact on student learning.

2. Plan for exchange visits among co-teachers. If your school has an extensive co-teaching program, arrange for novices to observe in veterans' classroom. If your program is relatively new, perhaps you could arrange to visit co-taught classrooms in a neighboring school or district.

3. If you cannot arrange for classroom visits, consider having each partnership in your school video record a co-taught lesson, editing the video to focus on its highlights. Co-teachers then could watch the videos, with the teachers who made the recording explaining and critiquing their lesson and colleagues making suggestions and discussing how to apply the information to their own lessons.

References

Friend, M., & Cook, L. (2013). *Interactions: Collaboration skills for school professionals* (7th edition). Upper Saddle River, NJ: Pearson/Allyn & Bacon.

Friend, M., Cook, L., Hurley-Chamberlain, D., & Shamberger, C. (2010). Co-teaching: An Illustration of the complexity of collaboration in special education. *Journal of Educational & Psychological Consultation, 20,* 9-27.

Gurgur, H., & Uzuner, Y. (2011): Examining the implementation of two co-teaching models: Team teaching and station teaching. *International Journal of Inclusive Education, 15,* 589-610.

Sileo, J. M., & van Garderen, D. (2010). Opportunities to learn mathematics: Blending co-teaching structures with research-based practices. *Teaching Exceptional Children, 42*(3), 14-21.

Chapter 4 Appendix

The forms included on the following pages were referenced in this chapter. They are included in the order in which they were mentioned and are intended to assist you in thinking about co-teaching approaches and applying them to your co-teaching situation.

Tracking Small-Group Student Participation
in Alternative Teaching

This form enables co-teachers to keep track over time of which students have been in a small group and for what purpose. You could create a similar form on a spreadsheet.

	Date, Purpose of the Small Group, and Teacher Leading It									
Student Name										

From Isolation to Partnership: Applying Co-Teaching Approaches

You may be most accustomed to thinking about teaching as an endeavor in which one person leads. If you are a veteran teacher, you probably have many ideas and patterns that you use to be an effective teacher. As you read about the co-teaching approaches, use this form to re-design a specific lesson to incorporate each approach. Complete each section for a one-teacher lesson and then jot options for changing the lesson plan to take advantage of the talents of two teachers.

Subject_____ Date_____

Topic/Lesson_____

Competencies/Objectives/Standards

_____
_____
_____
_____
_____

Materials

_____
_____
_____
_____
_____

Student Special Needs

_____
_____
_____
_____
_____

(continued on next page)

	One Teacher Lesson	Co-Taught Lesson Approach _____
Anticipatory Set		
Procedures		
Independent Practice		
Closure		
Assessment		
Accommodations and modifications for students with disabilities or other special needs		
Notes		

Survey on Co-Teaching Approaches

Use this survey to have co-teachers estimate the proportion of their shared time they use each approach. What do the results suggest in terms of areas for discussion and growth?

Actual %	Ideal %	
_____	_____	**One Teaching, One Observing.** In this co-teaching approach, more detailed observation of students engaged in the learning process can occur. Co-teachers decide in advance what types of specific observational information to gather during instruction and agree on a system for gathering the data. Afterward, the teachers analyze the information together and use it to plan instruction.
_____	_____	**Station Teaching.** In this co-teaching approach, teachers divide content and students. Each teacher then instructs one group and subsequently repeats the instruction for the other group. If appropriate, a third "station" gives students an opportunity to work independently or with a student leader. As appropriate, even more stations are formed.
_____	_____	**Parallel Teaching.** On occasion, students' learning would be greatly facilitated if they just had more supervision by the teacher or more opportunity to respond. In parallel teaching, the teachers are both teaching the same information, but they divide the class group and do so simultaneously. The approach also may be used to group students by skills levels or to present differing perspectives or points of view.
_____	_____	**Alternative Teaching.** In most class groups, occasions arise in which several students need specialized attention. In alternative teaching, one teacher takes responsibility for the large group while the other works with a smaller group (for example, re-teaching, pre-teaching, providing enrichment, assessing).
_____	_____	**Teaming.** In teaming, both teachers are delivering the same instruction at the same time. Some teachers refer to this as having "one brain in two bodies." Most co-teachers consider this approach the most complex but satisfying way to co-teach, but it is the approach that is most dependent on teachers' styles and sense of partnership.
_____	_____	**One Teaching, One Assisting.** In this approach to co-teaching one person retains primary responsibility for teaching while the other professional circulates through the room providing unobtrusive assistance to students as needed.
100%	**100%**	**TOTAL**

If you'd like to make additional comments about co-teaching approaches in our school, please use the reverse side. Thanks for participating.

Chapter 5
Instructional Quality in Co-Teaching

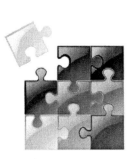

What office is there which involves more responsibility,
which requires more qualifications, and which ought, therefore,
to be more honorable than teaching?
~Harriet Martineau

Learner Objectives

1. Analyze the meanings of common instructional terms (for example, differentiation, accommodation) and explain their application for co-teaching.

2. Assess the extent to which your current or planned co-teaching practices incorporate specially designed instruction, describing a sample lesson that illustrates your increased knowledge of how to do this.

3. Critique various methods used to evaluate and assign grades for the learning of students with special needs in general education settings, reviewing your own practices and examining whether they should be adjusted for co-teaching.

We are in the middle of a perfect instructional storm. The pressure to improve student outcomes, including reducing the achievement gap between typical students and those with special needs, is greater than ever. At the same time, teachers are being challenged to significantly change their instructional approaches using the principles of the Common Core State Standards. Simultaneously, professionals have recognized that in order for students with special needs to reach their potential, they should in most cases receive their educational services alongside their typical peers, leading to an increased emphasis on co-teaching. And just in case the situation was not complex enough, next-generation teacher evaluation systems are raising many questions about how to assign student learning outcomes to teacher performance ratings and, in some cases, teachers' financial compensation. In the midst of all these changes, co-teachers are engaged in the daily joys and challenges of meeting the needs of all their diverse learners.

The goal of this chapter is not to provide simplistic answers to the many instructional dilemmas facing co-teachers, nor is it designed to be a list of instructional strategies to be used in the classroom. The former tactic would be unethical, and the latter approach would be duplicating the hundreds upon hundreds of books and other publications that outline evidence-based instructional strategies, examples of which are included in the appendix for this chapter. Instead, the purpose here is to carefully examine what instruction in a co-taught class must include in order for it to be a defensible service delivery option for students with disabilities or other special needs.

Instructional Vocabulary and Co-Teaching

In speaking with co-teachers across the country and around the world, I often ask them how their co-taught class is substantively different from a solo-taught class, other than the obvious fact that two teachers are participating in the delivery of instruction. Before you read further, how would you and your co-teacher answer that question, whether based on your current or planned practices? The array of answers falls along a continuum that includes these points:

- *We have clearly been told that the students in the class must meet the same standards and pass the same test as all the other students. Therefore, it is not appropriate to make any changes for them, and it would not be fair to the other students. If students with special needs are assigned to the class, they should be able to do the work. If they cannot, they should not have been placed here.*

- *Our co-teaching has had a strong positive impact on the entire class. When we co-teach, all of our students have access to more help so that they are better able to succeed. Having two sets of hands in the classroom is unquestionably beneficial.*

- *We find that in our co-taught class, we are able to differentiate for all our students. We can provide extra assistance to the students who need it and can make adjustments for others. Working together, we do a much better job reaching our students' needs than either of us could do alone.*

- *The goal of having the specialist in our class is to be sure that the identified students receive the supports that they need. The specialist (whether a special educator or an ESL teacher) can get around to those students to be sure they are comprehending, but she also may support other students who are struggling.*

♣ *The students in our co-taught class (with disabilities) need a variety of accommodations. The special educator knows what those accommodations are and makes sure that students receive them. That helps the students to be able to complete the assignments and activities that are part of this class.*

Was your response similar to any of these comments? Would you be surprised to learn that none of these responses about the instructional uniqueness of co-teaching is an adequate answer, even if you're trying your best as a co-teacher? Let's briefly examine what each of these statements implies, using the discussion as a foundation for understanding the instructional expectations in a co-taught class.

No Changes Allowed

As part of the strong movement to hold all students to the same high academic standards, a "no exceptions" approach to co-teaching is understandable, but completely unacceptable. This mentality overlooks the fact that students with special needs would not have that designation if they did not need something different in relation to their instruction. For all but students with significant intellectual disabilities the standards are the same. However, some type of adjustment is an inherent component of special education or ESL services.

Extra Help

A special education director was recently accompanying me on co-taught classroom visits. We observed a class in which the general educator led all the instruction while the special educator walked around helping students. At the end of the session, the director remarked that if she divided the special educator's salary by the proportion of the school day spent in that role, she was paying a teacher about $12,000/year to be a classroom helper for that single class period, a situation she considered an intolerable waste of personnel funds. Her comments were harsh, but they make an excellent point. The purpose of assigning two professionals to a single class is to ensure that specific instructional responsibilities are completed. If "help" is all that is needed, a volunteer, university intern, or even an older student tutor could be assigned to support the class.

Differentiation

Differentiation is a term that has been used so extensively to describe so many educational practices that it has lost some of its technical meaning. Experts on differentiation generally consider it a framework for making instructional adjustments in order to better meet student needs, including changes in content, the teaching/learning process, the products students produce, and the learning environment (e.g., Roe, 2010; Tomlinson & Imbeau, 2012). Given this definition, it might appear that differentiation would be an appropriate goal for co-teachers. It is, but it is not enough. ALL teachers should differentiate for students, whether they are teaching alone or teaching with a colleague. Although it is true that co-teachers often can provide more differentiation than solo teachers, if differentiation is their primary or sole purpose, students with special needs still are not receiving the specialized instruction to which they are entitled.

Individualized Support

Some co-teachers suggest that the key difference between a one-teacher and a two-teacher class is the individual support to targeted students. Sometimes specialists will refer to being sure that "their" students are closely monitored. Sometimes general educators will express relief that the specialist is able provide this support, especially in a crowded class of students with diverse needs. As with the "help" example above, this is an inadequate instructional change in the class. It is a form of one-to-one differentiation, acceptable but not sufficient.

Accommodations

The term *accommodation* is directly related to special education (and also students who have Section 504 plans). An accommodation comprises the tools students need in order to acquire information and skills, retain them, and demonstrate their learning through activities or assessments. That is, accommodations are "work arounds" that enable students to learn, a concept also applicable to English language learners. You are probably familiar with many types of accommodations, including testing in a small, structured environment; reduced assignment length (without removing core content); and use of technology such as a digital audio recorder or speech-to-text translation software. The dilemma is that accommodations are designed to enable students to succeed in the general education setting; they generally do not require the ongoing participation of a specialist. That is, while specialists are charged with creating accommodations based on student assessed needs and ensuring these supports are available, general educators are the professionals who usually implement the accommodations. Co-teaching should not be needed for the delivery of accommodations. Further, if student needs can be met strictly through the use of accommodations, the student should not need special education (or other special services) in that instructional setting.

Are you perhaps wondering where this discussion is headed? It does have a point: Whether you are learning about co-teaching for possible future practice, just beginning your co-teaching journey, or a veteran teaching partner, you must understand that, no matter how well-intentioned and effective your efforts in other ways, the goal of having two educators in a classroom is not to accomplish a vague promise of extra assistance. Instead, it is to guarantee that the mandated services to which students with special needs assigned to the class are entitled are effectively provided.

Specially Designed Instruction

The above discussion of what is not adequate and what is not acceptable instructional practice in co-teaching is the basis for considering what the instruction *should* encompass, and Figure 5.1 is a summary of the dimensions along which it could vary. Along those dimensions, instruction in a co-taught class should meet all the standards set for today's classroom: It should be rigorous, grounded in the Common Core (in nearly all states), and based on student assessment data. In addition, it should reflect evidence-based approaches, and it should be differentiated to address the diversity of needs among the students in the class. However, for students with disabilities (and in a more general sense, English language learners and other students with special needs), the instruction also must be designed specifically to address the characteristics and identified needs that led to them being eligible for special education or other services.

Definition of Specially Designed Instruction (SDI)

When a student is identified as eligible for special education, that student is entitled to receive three types of services (Friend & Bursuck, 2014):

1. Special education, which is defined as specially designed instruction

2. Related services (for example, speech/language therapy, physical therapy), as needed, and

3. Supplementary aids and services, which are the supports that enable a student to meaningfully participate in the general education setting and may include accommodations, modifications (for students with significant intellectual disabilities), assistive technology, professional development for the teachers working with the student, and many others.

It is the first item — specially designed instruction — that is the heart of special education and must be the starting point for any discussion about instruction in co-taught classes. If co-teaching is determined to be the best service delivery option, that is, the best vehicle through which a student will receive (at least for

Figure 5.1
Dimensions for Instructional Adjustments

Dimension	Explanation
Pre-instruction	Strategies for assessment of prerequisite skills and match between student learning status and upcoming instruction; planning so that instruction is deliberate; analysis of strategies for embedding IEP or ILP goals into instruction
Content, materials, technology	Books, alternative, and other print materials, manipulatives, assistive and instructional technology that may be part of SDI or form accommodations; for students with significant intellectual disabilities, alignment of standard curriculum with student goals
Environment	Physical setting, furniture, lighting, classroom climate, availability of supplies, and so on
Content structure and delivery	Strategies for large-group and small-group instruction as well as direct and explicit approaches
Student engagement and learning	Strategies for student participation and practice (e.g., peer mediated instruction), across all modalities and with variations in frequency and intensity
Student evaluation	Strategies for determining student progress in learning, whether on daily work, for the purpose of monitoring progress on IEP or ILP goals, or for summative evaluation
Collaboration among adults	Consultation, co-teaching, support from paraprofessionals or other specialists, teaming, and other strategies for blending professional expertise to meet student needs

that subject area or course) special education, then it is the responsibility of the special educator to provide specially designed instruction during that time period.

Specially designed instruction (SDI) is defined as appropriate changes to the content (for some students), methodology, or delivery of instruction so that it is explicitly linked to the eligible student's present level of performance, specifically in the area(s) of disability, and the resulting IEP goals. For students who are ELLs, it directly relates to their individual learning plans (ILPs). SDI should be intentional and systematic, carefully planned, and closely monitored for its impact on student learning. It is unique to the student and should have as a goal enabling the student to access and achieve the standards established in the general curriculum. Finally, SDI is characterized as requiring the assessment, teaching, and evaluation knowledge and skills of the special educator or other specialist.

Notice that this definition of SDI extends the discussion in Chapter 3 about professional roles. When a general education teacher is instructing a group of students that includes those with disabilities, that educator may be providing accommodations and should be differentiating. However, in nearly every state (but not all) that teacher is not required to provide specially designed instruction — that is the responsibility of the special educator. The co-teaching time is the period during which specially designed instruction is delivered.

Understanding the technical aspects of SDI also clarifies why assertions about help, support, accommodations, and perceived benefits of co-teaching are insufficient. In some ways, co-teaching is the most sophisticated type of teaching there could be, because it requires that professionals deliver the standard curriculum while embedding specially designed instruction to address in a respectful and non-stigmatizing way students' special instructional needs (Friend & Cook, 2013).

The fact that SDI must be tailored to an eligible student's assessed needs and IEP or individual learning plan (ILP) goals does not mean that no other student may benefit from the instruction. In fact, co-teachers often report that a strategy implemented for one student was very beneficial for several other students in the class. The students are receiving what is sometimes called incidental benefit from the specially designed instruction. However, for students with disabilities, if co-teachers find themselves thinking that everything they do for students with disabilities is beneficial for all students, one of two questions must be raised: Are the students with disabilities truly receiving specially designed instruction? or Should the students have a disability designation if what they need are strategies that should be available to all students?

When professionals describe specially designed instruction, several common characteristics often are mentioned (e.g., Kennedy, Lloyd, Cole, & Ely, 2012). For example, the instruction usually is designed after a careful analysis of the student's current level of learning (for example, a pretest has indicated that the student lacks several prerequisite skills to learn the material in the new unit); potential gaps (for example, the reading level of the upcoming material is more than three years higher than the student's current level); and characteristics as a learner (for example, the student has been determined to have a significant problem with short term memory and processes language at an exceptionally slow pace). The instruction also usually should be direct and explicit, that is, teachers provide in a careful step-by-step manner the knowledge to be acquired or skill to be learned. A third characteristic of SDI is that it generally provides more opportunities for practice that typically would be needed by other students.

Perhaps the most important conversations that co-teachers are having concern specially designed instruction — what it is, who it should benefit, how it aligns with the district's articulated curriculum goals or standards, what it looks like in the classroom, and how its provision is documented and monitored. In the following sections several examples of SDI are provided to facilitate your discussion of this most critical dimension of co-teaching.

SDI Examples for Academics

IEPs for students with disabilities generally address academic needs because eligibility requires that the disability is having a negative impact on student educational performance. The challenge for co-teachers is to incorporate these goals into the grade level curriculum. The following examples illustrate the type of thinking that is required, but the blending of curriculum standards, SDI, and co-teaching approaches has endless variations.

Third grade student whose reading is not fluent. Corey's reading is painfully slow, word-by-word, and expressionless. Although he knows the meanings of individual words, his comprehension often seems to be affected by the laborious process of pronouncing each word and finishing each sentence. Fluency is addressed on his IEP. In the co-taught class, providing Corey with instruction on fluency is a current priority. The teachers accomplish this in several ways. First, when they are station teaching, they sometimes have one teacher modeling fluent reading, followed by assisted reading in which selected students read out loud simultaneously with the teacher. When students have individually assigned work at an independent station, Corey often uses headphones at the computer for additional modeling and assisted reading practice. Twice each week, a university intern also is present in the classroom. One activity assigned to her is repeated readings. That is, she is provided with a list of students who should be called to her work station so that the week's literature can be read a second or third time. The special educator is checking Corey's fluency once every two weeks, gathering data on his words correctly read per minute.

Seventh grade students with math disabilities learning about functions. Four students in the co-taught math class have identified needs related to math, but all are expected to master the same standards as other students. The topic of functions has already been addressed, with the teachers teaming to demonstrate what functions are by forming a "function machine" in which specific input leads to specific output, based on the function. Students now are expected to apply that knowledge to a set of written problems. The teachers arrange the students for "triple parallel" teaching. The worksheets students have all look about the same, but advanced students have a set of problems that require them to go beyond the basic functions information just presented. They are working as an independent group to identify the input for the function rather than the output, and they have to complete several examples for each problem to demonstrate that their answers are correct. The second group is working with one teacher who is responding to questions and guiding student work. The third group, consisting of 6 students (the 4 with IEPs and two others) and led by the other teacher, is reviewing step-by-step what a function is and how to determine output based on a function and given specific input. Then the students complete more practice on functions by acting them out. They then work with a partner to solve several problems related to functions. The next day, these students complete yet more practice as an alternative to the warm-up activity other students are assigned.

Tenth grade student who struggles to remember vocabulary in U.S. history. Annie has a learning disability, and she has an extraordinarily difficult time learning the many vocabulary words in her U.S. History class. The unit on WWI alone includes 40 key terms. The co-teachers often spend a small part of the block-scheduled course parallel teaching in order to foster discussion; vocabulary instruction is often embedded in the discussions. For Annie, the teachers ensure that the word is used in an appropriate context and that Annie has the opportunity to use the word several times as part of the lesson, both evidence-based approaches for teaching vocabulary. They also ensure that words are reviewed each day, often using a quick re-teaching strategy for this purpose or using technology at an independent station for the needed practice for several students, including Annie, another student who seems very unsure of herself, and three English language learners. When the teachers team, they sometimes embed additional vocabulary instruction: The special educator will initiate a game of stump the students and insert vocabulary questions. Although a number of students benefit from this strategy, it was put in place as another way to offer Annie additional practice. Finally, the teachers use an on-line system for assigning and collecting homework. Because they can have different students have different assignments, Annie sometimes is assigned vocabulary practice instead of other work.

SDI Examples for Behavior

Co-teachers sometimes note that they are comfortable providing specially designed instruction as part of co-teaching, but they express concern that some students exhibit behaviors that make their participation in a general education classroom distracting and sometimes disruptive. Other students are so withdrawn or disengaged that teachers question whether the students are benefitting from the class. Students whose present level of performance indicates that behaviors are a significant concern may be entitled to specially designed instruction to reduce inappropriate behaviors, increase appropriate behaviors, and, most importantly, learn strategies to avoid behavior problems. As with academics, the number of examples that could be provided is as diverse as the number of students in co-taught classes. The following samples are intended to illustrate how behavior-based specially designed instruction might occur during co-teaching.

Fourth grade student who easily becomes frustrated when work assigned is difficult. Robert is eligible for special education services as having a mild intellectual disability. He has a behavior intervention plan (BIP) because of his extraordinarily disruptive behavior when he is frustrated. For example, last week during math, he tried for approximately 25 seconds to begin his work. He then pushed it off his desk, threw his pencil toward the wastebasket, put his head down on his desk, and refused teacher direction to raise it, loudly saying many times, "No, no, no!" One behavior goal on Robert's IEP concerns learning to express frustration in words and asking for assistance instead of becoming upset.

To address this goal, the co-teachers have embedded in their language arts instruction a station, led by the special educator, in which students write stories about getting frustrated and what they do to feel less frustrated and deal with the situations. The discussion, facilitated by teacher, includes questions specifically intended to provide Robert with simple instruction on strategies he should use. As other students begin writing and illustrating their examples and responses, the special educator works with Robert on a specific strategy, a script to follow when frustrated by school work. The students, including Robert, then act out their scenarios. Before the end of the class, the special educator asks another student to role play Robert's scenario a second time. This practice occurs several more times, and both teachers also cue Robert to use the strategy when given challenging work. The teachers also verbally praise him for using it. They also note each time he uses (and does not use) the strategy. Although all students participated in a writing activity related to frustration, the specially designed instruction for Robert was much more detailed, occurred over several days, and its impact was documented. It also will be reviewed on a regular basis over several weeks until Robert is using the strategy consistently and effectively.

Ninth grade student who is off-task or inattentive. Ciara has a behavior disability and used to receive most of her education in a separate setting. In this first year in high school, however, she is assigned to a co-taught English class. Data indicate that she is off-task so often that she undoubtedly is missing key instruction. Recent observations found her off-task an average of 65 percent of the time, and her behaviors included applying make-up, chatting with students seated nearby, sitting with her head down and her hoodie over it, and sitting still, staring, while other students were taking notes or participating in small-group discussions. One of her IEP goals is to learn metacognitive skills to monitor her attending behavior in order to increase it. As part of co-teaching, Ciara's teachers have been teaching metacognitive skills, modeling what a student's brain should be saying during instruction, and the teachers are to the point in the instructional sequence that they are asking students to demonstrate what to do. Ciara is assigned to be a leader for this ongoing activity, and both teachers contribute to coaching her as she demonstrates these skills. She also has an individually designed behavior contract as part of the class, and she earns an exemption on a small amount of homework when her on-task rate of behavior is progressively higher from week to week, a reward she selected. Occasionally, when the teachers are conferencing with individual students (using a variation of alternative teaching), the special educator provides additional instruction related to self-talk as a metacognitive strategy.

SDI Examples for Social Skills

For some students with disabilities, social skills are an important part of their learning goals. Just like academic skills and appropriate behavior, social skills must be addressed in the co-taught class by providing the specially designed instruction that will lead to the student reaching his or her IEP goals.

A first grade student with a learning disability and a behavior disorder with social skills deficits. Based on observations and interviews, Emma's IEP team determined that she has significant social skills deficits. That is, when she grabs a toy another child is playing with, pushes her way into a game without asking, or calls other students names, it is because she does not know the appropriate ways to interact with peers. As part of planning at the beginning of the year, the co-teachers reviewed Emma's IEP goals related to social skills, and based on the special educator's judgment, are first focusing on making positive rather than negative remarks to classmates. They are embedding this skill instruction throughout co-taught lessons, and the general education teacher is continuing practice on social skills even when teaching alone. For example, while teaming, the teachers modeled being positive regarding each other. They then asked students to react to their behavior, and they made sure Emma was an active participant in this exercise. The teachers also use partner learning activities, and they begin each one with students saying "something nice" about the other, monitoring Emma and coaching her if she seems unsure what to say. The teachers also are diligent to "catch" Emma using this social skill, verbally reinforcing her use of positive words with classmates. In fact, the special educator has observed Emma initiating these behaviors at least eight times in the past week, and so the co-teachers are planning to add a second social skill to this embedded instruction. They plan, though, to continue reinforcing Emma's use of positive comments to peers and to periodically gather data to ensure she is maintaining this skill.

An eighth grade student with autism spectrum disorder (ASD) needs to participate in conversations about non-preferred topics and to take turns in conversation. Scott has a wealth of knowledge on several topics, including nearly every detail regarding China's Terracotta Warriors. As is typical of some students with autism, though, he often does not realize that others do not want to repeatedly hear about this current favorite topic of discussion. Similarly, he often does not remember that in a conversation people take turns speaking. Goals related to these skills are part of Scott's IEP. In the co-taught class, Scott's teachers sometimes use parallel teaching combined with observing. That is, they split the group in half so each of the teachers is responsible for just part of the students. They then partner the students, assigning them discussion topics. For Scott, this procedure was taught using a social story, introduced one day as other students completed an assignment that Scott had finished very quickly. The teacher monitors Scott's conversation closely and uses a visual signal if he is not taking turns or if he suddenly switches the topic to the Terracotta Warriors. As students transition back to the large group, the teacher touches base with him to be sure he understood the need to "let go." With teacher guidance, Scott is beginning to monitor his own behavior and judge his own progress.

English Language Learners and SDI

This discussion of specially designed instruction has focused on students with disabilities because special education law explicitly includes specially designed instruction as a requirement of services, and so the concept is most immediately applicable to them. However, English language learners also must receive services, and when those services are provided in the context of a co-taught class, the notion that the instruction necessary should be based on students' individual learning plans is comparable. That is, when an ESL teacher is co-teaching, the goal of the partnership is not for general assistance or translation. Instead, it is intended to implement whatever strategies will directly and explicitly enable the targeted students to become proficient in English, whether that is through the provision of sheltered English, explicit instruction in academic vocabulary, and/or scaffolding students' learning when they lack the experiences that may be necessary for upcoming lessons.

Evaluation of Student Learning

The companion topic to appropriately instructing students in co-taught classes is the evaluation of their learning (e.g., O'Connor, 2010; Wormelli, 2006). Grading day-to-day student work in co-taught classes sometimes is a matter of controversy and conflict, and no single solution to the grading dilemma exists. Similar debates occur when teachers are making decisions about grades for report cards. What is most important is that the approach to grading is fair but at the same time considers students' special needs (Silva, Munk, & Bursuck, 2005). In this section a few of the most important points about assessment and grading are offered as a means to foster your own conversations on this important topic.

Assessment of Day-to-Day Student Work

Co-teachers (and other educators, for that matter) should keep in mind these points for assessing the day-to-day work of students with disabilities and other special needs:

1. More than 80 percent of students with disabilities do not have intellectual disabilities, and so they are capable of learning the standard curriculum, albeit with specialized instruction and accommodations as needed. Further, nearly all students are expected to take the standard high-stakes tests (exceptions being students with significant intellectual disabilities and early English learners).

2. The goal throughout instruction should be to provide accommodations for students (that is, the tools so students can more readily learn, defined earlier in this chapter), along with needed specialized instruction. For students with disabilities and those who have Section 504 plans, accommodations are formally documented. Modifications (that is, eliminating parts of the general curriculum standards or competencies) should be avoided unless the student has a significant intellectual disability, in which case what is taught should be aligned with the general curriculum. Modifications also are documented on IEPs.

3. Discussions about students' required accommodations should occur prior to instruction, preferably before the beginning of co-teaching, and should be reviewed at least once each grading period. Co-teachers should be clear on the accommodations (and modifications, for a few students) required and their impact on the evaluation of student work and progress.

4. Co-teachers also should clarify what the curricular standards require versus what students traditionally have been asked to do. In many cases, there are multiple ways to demonstrate achievement of a standard, and students with special needs may need to use an alternative to the approaches used with other students.

5. When students receive accommodations there should be no negative impact on their daily grades. That is, if a tool helps a student to learn or demonstrate learning, but the curriculum access is the same as for other students, that student earns the same grades as other students. A simple example includes writing bullet points instead of paragraphs on a high school civics test. Unless the skill being addressed was paragraph-writing, reducing the complexity of the task by allowing the use of bullet points should not result in a decision

that the student, for example, cannot earn an "A." However, when work is modified, grades may be affected because the standard has been lowered significantly by reducing what the student is responsible for learning.

6. Some teachers count students' in-class work and homework more than tests because the students are diligent but do not perform well on tests. Other teachers do just the opposite, minimizing the grades for homework for students who do well on tests but who seldom complete homework. Yet other teachers create options for students to earn extra credit to make up for missed assignments and poor test scores. As with many other parts of instruction, co-teachers should discuss what strategies fit the entire class and which are only available to students with disabilities by virtue of their status as protected by special education law.

7. Some teachers decide that, instead of making changes in assignments and activities, they will simply lower their grading scale. This is not a particularly appropriate strategy. It would be better to adjust the work so that the student is able to more readily access it, keeping the assessment of the work consistent with procedures used for all students. Simply lowering the grading scale does not communicate that appropriate tools have been put in place to support student learning.

Above all, co-teachers should ensure that they both understand how the work of students with special needs will be assessed. They then should clarify that information with students and students' parents. In all cases, they should always reflect on the balance between holding students to the highest standards while acknowledging that adjustments in instructional and assessment procedures will be necessary.

Report Card Grades

If co-teachers have careful discussions about the assessment of students' day-to-day work, many of the issues that sometimes surround report-card grading will have been raised. This is important for students with disabilities because of implications for services and legal issues, but it is also essential for ELLs, particularly because clear district or school grading policies are much less likely to be in place for them. For example, in some school districts, report cards at the elementary level are based on grade level standards. Co-teachers worry that this may mean students will always be rated at a very low level, even if making significant progress, because they are working below grade level, a problem that often occurs for reading and sometimes math. Teaching partners should discuss this dilemma prior to beginning instruction, determining which standards may be met through accommodations, so that student progress is accurately communicated. They also should create a plan for the specially designed instruction that will foster accelerated student learning so that the gap is reduced.

In another example, in some high schools grades for certain courses are directly associated with performance on high stakes testing. If a small percentage of the final grade for the course is thus designated, it should not be a problem. However, if a significant part of the grade is based on that single assessment, the IEP team may need to discuss whether some type of accommodation should be documented, and ESL professionals may want to propose alternatives for some students. At all grade levels, co-teachers should discuss other progress monitoring procedures (required for students with IEPs); these may allow students' progress to be clearly explained, even though the standard report card indicates that the curriculum is modified or the student is not reaching the standard.

When considered across grade levels, report cards serve different purposes. At the elementary and middle school levels, they are a mechanism for information sharing among teachers, students, and parents. Thus, the goal at these levels is to ensure clear communication. At the high school level, grades are still a communication tool, but the recipients expand to include potential employers and post-secondary education institutions. Thus, grades must accurately convey students' achievement, neither artificially inflating it nor artificially depressing it just because of the presence of a disability.

For Further Thought

1. What instructional vocabulary typically is used in your school when discussing students with disabilities, English language learners, or other students with special needs? Why is it critical to understand the technical meanings of this terminology and to use it accurately?

2. Using the definition provided in this chapter, what are at least 3-5 examples of specially designed instruction for your students? To what extent have these been embedded in the activities of your co-taught class? How is it possible to balance the need for SDI with the goal of avoiding stigmatizing students?

3. What grading practices are outlined in your school or school district policy? What additional guidelines have been set by your grade level, team, or department? How might these policies and guidelines assist or inadvertently harm students with disabilities or other special needs? How should you and your co-teacher grade your students with special needs?

Taking Action

1. Design, implement, and evaluate a 30-minute professional development at your school regarding instruction for students with disabilities, those who are English language learners, and those with other special needs. Emphasize what students are entitled to receive, what this means for instruction in co-taught classes, and how it might affect grading practices.

2. Using a week's lesson plans, the information contained in Figure 5.1, and the IEPs or ILPs for your students, annotate the lesson plans to demonstrate how specially designed instruction will occur as part of co-teaching. Identify aspects of SDI that are challenging to embed, and discuss with your co-teacher how to address this need.

3. Arrange visits across co-taught classes among the teachers in your school. Have as an emphasis for the visits finding examples of how the classrooms are substantively different from solo-taught classes. After the visits, hold a meeting of all participants to discuss findings, celebrating positive examples and seeking ways to increase the number of examples. Focus discussion on ways to incorporate specially designed instruction into the teaching and learning process.

References

Friend, M., & Cook, L. (2013). *Interactions: Collaboration skills for school professionals* (7th edition). Upper Saddle River, NJ: Pearson/Allyn & Bacon.

Kennedy, M. J., Lloyd, J. W., Cole, M. T., & Ely, E. (2012). Specially designed vocabulary instruction in the content areas: What does high quality instruction look like? *Teaching Exceptional Children Plus*. Retrieved from http://tecplus.org/articles/article/1/0.

O'Connor, J. (2010). *Students with disabilities can met accountability standards: A roadmap for school leaders*. Lanham, MD: Rowman & Littlefield.

Roe, M. F. (2010). The ways teachers do the things they do: Differentiation in middle level literacy classes. *Middle Grades Research Journal, 5*, 139-152.

Silva, M., Munk, D.D., & Bursuck, W.D. (2005). Grading adaptations for students with disabilities. *Intervention in School and Clinic, 41*, 87-98.

Tomlinson, C., & Imbeau, M. B. (2012). Common sticking points about differentiation. *School Administrator, 69*(5), 18-22.

Wormelli, R. (2006). *Fair isn't always equal: Assessing and grading in the differentiated classroom*. Westerville, OH: National Middle School Association.

Chapter 5 Appendix

The appendix for Chapter 5 contains two sets of resources that might be helpful as you address the critical questions of ensuring that instruction is appropriate. The first item is a list of books on teaching students with special needs in general education settings. You should also scan professional journals for information on this topic, as there are a nearly unlimited number of articles written, some with a research base and some based on authors' experiences. The second resource is a listing of websites that have thousands of ideas and additional links related to instruction for students with disabilities and other special needs to ensure meaningful participation and success in general education settings.

A Selection of Books of Academic and Behavior Strategies and Interventions

Bender, W. N. (2012). *Differentiating instruction for students with learning disabilities: New best practices for general and special educators* (3rd edition). Thousand Oaks, CA: Corwin.

Brownell, M. T., Smith, S. J., Crockett, J. B., & Griffin, C. C. (2012). *Inclusive instruction: Evidence-based practices for teaching students with disabilities (what works for special-needs learners).* New York, NY: Guilford Press.

Cipani, E. (2011). *Decoding challenging classroom behaviors: What every teacher and paraeducator should know!* Springfield, IL: Charles C. Thomas.

Dove, M. G., & Honigsfeld, A. (2013). *Common core for the not-so-common learner, Grades K-5: English language arts.* Thousand Oaks, CA: Corwin.

Friend, M., & Bursuck, W. D. (2014). *Including students with special needs: A practical guide for classroom teachers* (7th edition). Upper Saddle River, NJ: Pearson/Merrill.

Gregory, G. H., & Chapman, C. M. (2012). *Differentiated instructional strategies: One size doesn't fit all* (3rd edition). Thousand Oaks, CA: Corwin.

Hall, T. E., Meyer, A., & Rose, D. H. (Eds.). (2012). *Universal design for learning in the classroom: Practical applications (what works for special-needs learners).* New York, NY: Guilford Press.

Heacox, D. (2002). *Differentiating instruction in the regular classroom: How to reach and teach all learners, grades 3-12.* Minneapolis, MN: Free Spirit Publishing.

Leon-Guerrero, R. M., Matsumoto, C., & Martin, J. (2011). *Show ME the data!: Data-based instructional decisions made simple and easy.* Overland Park, KS: Autism Asperger Publishing.

Shea, T. M., & Bauer, A. M. (2012). *Behavior management: A practical approach for educators* (10th edition). Upper Saddle River, NJ: Pearson/Merrill.

Sprick, R. (2008). *Discipline in the secondary classroom: A positive approach to behavior management* (2nd edition). San Francisco, CA: Jossey-Bass.

Storey, K., & Post, M. (2012). *Positive behavior supports in classrooms and schools: Effective and practical strategies for teachers and other service providers.* Springfield, IL: Charles C. Thomas.

Internet Resources on Effective Instruction

🧩 *abcteach*
http://www.abcteach.com/

Practical instructional materials such as writing prompts, graphic organizers, research formats, and portfolio forms for pre-K through high school. Clip art for developing original instructional materials, flashcards, options for designing an original crossword, shape book, word wall, word unscramble, word search, math worksheets, and Sudoku by using abctools. Everything is free!

🧩 *Behavior Advisor*
http://www.behavioradvisor.com/

Award-winning website that includes thousands of ideas and links for addressing student behavior problems, whether they are simple or complex. This is a site that is best visited when there is time to browse.

🧩 *The Center for Applied Special Technology*
http://www.cast.org

Helpful suggestions for the universal design of learning materials and teaching practices to reduce the need for developing special accommodations and modifications for individual students in general education classes.

🧩 *The Center for Effective Collaboration and Practice*
http://cecp.air.org

Federally funded organization designed to promote effective educational practices for students with emotional and behavior problems.

🧩 *Florida Inclusion Network*
http://www.floridainclusionnetwork.com/page265.aspx

A one-stop resource for a wide variety of information on inclusive schooling, with ideas for teachers, administrators, parents, and others.

🧩 *Graphing Made Easy*
http://www.oswego.edu/~mcdougal/web_site_4_11_2005/index.html

State University of New York at Oswego website with a simple spreadsheet that can be used to record academic or behavior data; site also has suggestions for customizing your charts

InterventionCentral.org
http://www.interventioncentral.org/htmdocs/interventions/cbmwarehouse.php

Many instructional materials for graphing scores, adjusting readabilities, implementing reading fluency/math computation probes, collecting CMB/CBA data, etc. In the section where you can adjust readabilities for individual readers, the computer automatically counts words per a page and per a row so that it saves teachers time to prepare for lessons or tests.

The Leon County (FL) Schools
http://www.tandl.leon.k12.fl.us/lang/DIindex.html

Fosters differentiated instruction at all grade levels; includes links to additional reading material and sample lesson plans that incorporate the principles of differentiating.

The National Center to Improve Practice in Special Education through Technology, Media, and Materials
http://www2.edc.org/ncip

Compiled information about technology, disabilities, and instructional practices through a broad range of resources. This site also provides opportunities for teachers to collaborate.

National Library for Virtual Manipulatives
http://nlvm.usu.edu/en/nav/vlibrary.html

Contains links to extensive collection of virtual manipulatives PreK-12. Topics include numbers and operations, geometry, algebra, measurement, and data analysis and probability.

Speaking of Speech
http://www.speakingofspeech.com/Lesson_Plans___Data_Form.html

A variety of downloadable data forms. They are designed specifically for speech-language therapists, but many of them also could be used by teachers to document specially designed instruction.

✦ Study Guides and Strategies
http://studygs.net

Provide study guides as well as strategies for preparing for and taking tests. The site provides study skills resources including several links to study skills guides and interactive tutorials. Materials are available in 25 different languages.

✦ Teach-nology
http://www.teach-nology.com/tutorials/teaching/differentiate/planning

Offers step-by-step instruction for planning differentiation in general education classrooms.

✦ Vaughn-Gross Center for Reading & Language Arts
http://www.meadowscenter.org/vgc/materials/

Housed at the University of Texas, providing information for improving the literacy skills of all students, but especially those with disabilities, English language learners, and students struggling to read.

✦ What Works Clearinghouse
http://ies.ed.gov/ncee/wwc/

Federal project that reviews recommended programs and practices to determine whether they have an evidence base. A great source for ensuring your instructional approaches are based on research.

Chapter 6
Planning and Other Co-Teaching Logistics

When there is no wind, row.
~Latin Proverb

Learner Objectives

1. Outline the components of a contemporary model for co-teaching planning.

2. Identify realistic strategies for obtaining planning time and a structured planning protocol to make best use of such time.

3. Regularly use alternative planning strategies, both those that are electronic and those that are on-the-spot.

4. Outline other logistics, usually addressed by school administrators, that affect co-teaching (for example, class composition and scheduling).

Many co-teachers explain that their partnerships are strong and collaborative. They also note that they are finding creative and effective ways to use their collective talents to educate their diverse student groups. They often note, though, that they are limited in what they can accomplish because of challenges related to the logistics that surround co-teaching (Kohler-Evans, 2006). That topic is the focus of this chapter. Time is addressed in detail, and other logistics matters, including scheduling, are only briefly addressed, not because they are insignificant but because they are the responsibility of administrators (not teachers) and require more detailed treatment that is possible in this manual.

A Contemporary Co-Teaching Planning Model

By far the most common dilemma expressed among teachers and administrators setting up or refining co-teaching programs is the challenge of arranging common planning time for co-teaching partners (Dieker & Murawski, 2003; Kilanowski-Press, Foote, & Rinaldo, 2010; Pearl, Dieker, & Kirkpatrick, 2012; Spencer, 2005). If you reflect on current practices, though, you may come to realize that other options could ease this co-teaching stressor.

The Dilemma

Certainly, co-teachers must have some time to discuss their instruction and the students for whom they are responsible. However, professionals sometimes are conceptualizing planning time in a way more consistent with the 1960s or 1970s.

For example, when I ask educators how much common planning time they think should be allocated for co-teaching, they often give responses like these:

- One planning period each day for each co-taught class
- One planning period each week with each teacher with whom I co-teach, or
- At least two hours per week, split among the co-teaching partners.

A few realists say this:

- Any amount that is more than I have right now... which is none!

If funding and staffing levels support frequently scheduled planning time at your school, you are in an extraordinary situation. However, in most schools these options are not realistic, or scheduled time is not available at all for co-teaching planning. Examples of dilemmas encountered even when shared planning time is arranged include these:

- In an elementary school, it is true that the special educator or ESL teacher is assigned to meet with one grade level for weekly common planning, but this is the general grade level planning time and planning specific to the co-taught reading classes is not usually a priority.

- In a middle school, team planning occurs when students attend fine arts and related non-core academic classes. Unfortunately, this is the only opportunity in the school day for some students to receive the supplemental specially designed instruction they need, and so special educators are not available for these planning sessions.

🧩 In a high school, the specialist is provided with common planning time with one co-teacher. Unfortunately, that specialist co-teaches with three other colleagues and has no time to collaborate with them.

🧩 Across school levels, school professionals report that when they have common planning time, they feel obligated to use it and so meet nearly every day. As a result other work that each professional needs to complete is left unfinished and often carried home at the end of the day.

These examples demonstrate that, even when sincere efforts are made to provide co-teachers with opportunities to meet, the conundrum of managing all the time-consuming details of being a teacher has no simple solution.

A Solution: Marilyn's Planning Model

Having huddled with administrators around a conference table scanning sample schedules and trying to fit together all the pieces of the puzzle (with one piece always left sticking out) and having scanned the wall-sized master schedules decorating a high school office while a principal said, "I just cannot work around all the 'givens' and still arrange co-teaching, planning," I decided a different way of thinking about planning time is more likely to lead to constructive solutions. First, if you analyze contemporary society, lack of time is one of its key characteristics, a dilemma for professionals in *every* field. Next, a logical question is this: How are other professions addressing the time squeeze? Most importantly, which of the ideas being used in other disciplines might work in education?

The result of this problem solving process is a new way of thinking about co-teaching planning time. It is a three part model with these components:

1. **Periodic face-to-face planning.** It is not that face-to-face planning is not important, it is that we need to shift our thinking about how much of this time it is reasonable to have and how it can be feasibly scheduled. In chatting with many school administrators, when I suggest that they quit trying to place common planning time in the master schedule and instead find a means to provide coverage for co-teachers for at least an hour (preferably a bit more) once every four weeks for *macro planning*, they usually pause then then agree that could definitely be arranged.

2. **Electronic planning.** Co-teachers should use electronic planning as a complement to their face-to-face planning. However, this does not mean sending each other random e-mails that often end up lost or inadvertently deleted. Nor does it mean counting on text messaging as a key planning tool.

So many electronic collaboration platforms exist through wikis that they have become an essential co-teaching planning mechanism.

3. **On-the-spot planning.** Even when face-to-face and electronic planning have been effectively used to prepare for co-teaching, plans sometimes go awry. Teachers get behind in terms of pacing, a special program leads to a shortened schedule, or one of the educators has been absent for two days for professional development. In these any many other cases, teachers need just a few minutes to touch base. If they have a prescribed procedure for students to follow while they briefly meet, they are able to get back on track while avoiding a loss of instructional time for students.

Each of these planning time components is described in more detail in the following sections.

Face-to-Face Planning

The face-to-face component of Marilyn's planning model has two parts. The first is to use creativity and diligence to find common planning time at least once every four weeks. The second component is to apply a structured planning protocol so that these precious minutes are used as effectively as possible.

Finding Common Planning Time

Here are ways that teachers and administrators are successfully creating opportunities for professionals to collaborate.

Early planning during the summer. Although slightly different from all the other ideas presented in this section, especially for new co-teachers, getting a head start on the school year by planning during the summer can be very effective. Often this time is at least two or three hours, and sometimes it may span a half day or more. During such time, co-teachers get to know each other, address how they will successfully launch their co-taught class, and sketch plans for the first month of school. Funding for this type of time often comes from IDEA or Title monies. Alternatively, it sometimes is funded through professional development or curriculum planning funds, or similar sources.

Compensated after-school planning. Once the school year begins, some professionals find the simplest solution for planning is to schedule it outside school hours — but to receive some type of compensation for this extra effort. Two options seem reasonable: (a) pay for off-contract work or (b) professional development credit accumulated across a school year. In the first option, co-teachers agree to meet for a specified amount of time per month on their own time — before or after school or on weekends. They may complete a simple form of some type to demonstrate accountability, and they receive pay for this time at their hourly stipend rate. The payment will not make much difference in teachers' overall income, but it is an acknowledgement that co-teachers have planning responsibilities that go beyond those of other teachers. The second option, professional development credit, is similar, but it enables co-teachers to receive credit for their planning. If a district requires that teacher acquire, say, 15 clock hours of professional development time to receive one credit, co-teachers could, over a semester or year, log their planning outside school hours on an accountability form documenting the time spent meeting and receive this credit. In districts striving to increase co-teaching, after-school planning sessions for credit are advertised to all personnel so that teachers can meet at an arranged location to share ideas as they plan. Sometimes the location for these sessions is changed from month to month to make it convenient for everyone.

Alternative use of professional time. Many school districts have several teacher professional development days scheduled across the school year. In some districts, co-teachers may opt to be exempt from any planned activity for a certain number of hours each time one of these days is on the calendar. The teachers use this time for planning. This option has the advantage of occurring during the day and eliminating the need for additional resources. However, depending on the topic of the staff development, missing part of it might be problematic.

Use of substitute teachers. Before the current era of school reform and accountability, placing substitute teachers in classrooms to free co-teachers for planning was relatively common. Now, though, this option has many drawbacks in addition to the obvious practical ones — finding skilled substitute teachers and the funding to pay them. Because of increasing achievement standards, many administrators are reluctant to permit teachers to miss instructional time in order to plan for co-teaching. In addition, teachers released for planning through substitute teachers must plan appropriate instructional activities for their students and then ensure, after the planning, that those activities were completed. Many teachers find it just is not worth the time required to use this option.

If substitute teachers seem viable to you, some suggestions can streamline this type of planning option. First, the co-teachers should agree they will share the sub. That is, one month the sub will cover for the general education teacher, and the special education teacher or ESL teacher will use already-assigned planning time or lunch time to meet. The next month, the sub will cover for the special education teacher, and the general education teacher will use assigned planning time. In this way, neither professional is required to miss too much time with students. Second, it sometimes is helpful to arrange for this option at the beginning of the school year so that a substitute knows in August that a particular date in September, October, November, and so on will be scheduled for this type of subbing; the person can reserve those dates for the school. At the same time, teachers then have a predictable schedule for macro-planning and can work out among themselves and with their administrator how best to use the substitute teacher's time. In some locales, substitute teachers who are present for teacher absence are expected to help with this type of coverage during the time that the absent teacher would have had planning time (that is, such subs generally are not entitled to planning time and can be asked to provide coverage for an additional class).

Collaboration among staff members. Finding common planning time can become much easier if everyone works together. For example, in some schools, principals and assistant principals agree to cover a class period each week or specific number of minutes for a co-teaching partnership needing planning time. One teacher uses assigned planning time and the other is released by the administrator or the coverage is provided during the time partners would be teaching together. Other personnel — counselors, school psychologists, and literacy coaches, for example — also could contribute small amounts of time to facilitate co-teaching planning. Principals and other school professionals who do not have assigned class groups certainly have busy schedules and many responsibilities, but this approach can foster a collaborative school culture, can permit those professionals to spend meaningful time in classrooms, and can help co-teachers to feel truly supported.

Other ways to collaborate for face-to-face planning time also can be worked out. For example, in some high schools teachers receive compensation for extra duties they complete, usually during their planning period. Thus, a teacher may be paid to release co-teachers so they can plan. In other schools, co-teachers are exempt from a duty, (hall duty, bus duty, study hall) so that they can find time to plan with their partner. In yet other schools, when more than one special education teacher is employed, the teachers may take turns covering classes for a general education teacher in order to create shared planning time (Dieker, 2007). That is, once every four weeks one of the teachers in a partnership covers for the teachers in another partnership. Those teachers either reciprocate, or they provide coverage for another partnership. The result is that a daisy chain of coverage occurs and all teachers get a planning time without the loss of a significant amount of instructional time.

Other shared planning time options. Creative administrators and other professionals have found many other strategies to arrange common planning time for co-teachers.

- Some elementary school principals are able to arrange for all the teachers in a grade level to have related arts (that is, art, music, physical education, library, technology) at one time. The specialist is also freed at this time. Once every four weeks, the co-teachers use this time for their specific planning while colleagues work on other grade level tasks.

🧩 In a few districts, the school calendar includes periodic days (as often as once per week or as seldom as once per grading period) designated for students' late arrival or early dismissal. In these schools, the standard school day is lengthened a bit, and then on the shortened days, students come late or leave early so professionals have additional time for professional development, conferences, and other essential activities. Co-teaching planning sometimes occurs during such times.

A Structured Planning Time Procedure

Regardless of how macro-planning time is arranged, the secret to success is using it wisely (Friend & Cook, 2013; Texas Education Agency, 2011). Think about what happens when you finally — after working with students all day — have a chance to interact with a colleague. Often a period of "venting and chatting" occurs. Teachers share their recollections about what occurred at last weekend's football game, or they spend a few minutes discussing other topics, such as the details of a recently seen movie or their own children's activities. Co-teachers must learn that any macro-planning meeting should have a clearly articulated agenda so that the precious shared time is spent on key topics.

Before and after the common planning session. As illustrated in Figure 6.1, this planning process requires that general educators come to the meeting prepared to discuss upcoming topics, projects, and activities. It is expected that they will spend a few minutes to gather needed guides or materials, refer to any required pacing guide, and otherwise ready themselves to explain to their co-teachers what will be covered. After the planning session, the specialists have the responsibility of mapping students' special needs onto the upcoming instruction, preparing any specialized materials, deciding on instructional approaches to facilitate students' understanding, and ensuring that students' learning goals are embedded within the planned curriculum.

The planning protocol. Figure 6.2 summarizes what should actually occur during the scheduled planning session. Note that the procedure is based on a full one-hour planning session. It would need to be adjusted if more or less time is available is. The protocol includes the following steps:

1. The general educator outlines the upcoming instruction. This might include briefly reviewing book chapter to be addressed, literature to be read, math concepts and skills to be introduced, projects to be initiated, science experiments or labs that are scheduled, and so on. The point is not

Figure 6.1
Overview of the Co-Teaching Planning Process

BEFORE THE MEETING

General education teacher gathers key information about upcoming curriculum, projects and activities, and other core content and brings this material to the meeting.

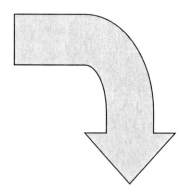

DURING THE MEETING

Using student data, general and special education or ESL teachers decide which to-teaching approaches to use given the curriculum to address, how to group students, which aspects of the instruction may pose difficulties, and which projects may be especially challenging for students. The meeting concludes with review and reflection on past instruction and the partnership.

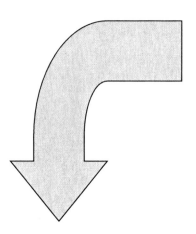

AFTER THE MEETING

Special education or ESL teacher prepares the unique differentiated materials and strategies necessary for the instruction, plans for meeting IEP goals or language-related goals within the curriculum, and prepares to incorporate learning process into the content.

to go through every detail. This step is in some ways a sort of sketch of the upcoming four weeks. The specialist will, individually, review the books or material and ask the general educator for clarification as needed. In the time allocated for this slot, general educators usually are surprised at how much information they can share.

2. Next, the two teachers should review student data so they have at their fingertips, before planning goes further, detailed information about students' learning status. Because teachers should be using student data on nearly a daily basis, the time allocated for this discussion is relatively brief. However, teachers should address topics such as trends in student learning, information about those who may lack prerequisite skills for the upcoming lessons, notations about students with some skills but also skill gaps, and so on.

3. Knowing the curriculum to be addressed and student learning status, the teachers should next discuss challenges students might encounter, material to be taught that may need to be covered in an especially careful way, and other ideas related to matching upcoming instruction to student learning status and needs. This conversation is intended to prepare the specialist for the after-session preparation of specially designed strategies, materials, and other means for ensuring students can learn with their peers.

4. With this information ready, teachers should then consider what their co-teaching might look like over the next four weeks. For example, they might decide that the vocabulary to be introduced is so extensive that they should plan to have a vocabulary station twice each week, with the specialist taking responsibility for that station. They also may decide that once each week for about half of their co-teaching time they will parallel teach because the planned instruction will be most effective if all students have increased opportunities to discuss the ideas presented. The goal of this discussion is to find at least one or two patterns that could be repeated over the next time period, thus facilitating the more detailed planning that will happen electronically. Some co-teachers find they can plan one-third or more of their co-teaching by thinking in terms of patterns in the instruction and how to apply the co-teaching approaches to those patterns.

5. Finally, whenever co-teachers have face-to-face planning time, they should reserve a few minutes to discuss their partnership, success from the past four weeks, issues encountered, or concerns either professional wishes to raise. The way to keep a professional relationship strong is to recognize that it is important to communicate about their classroom practices, the planning process being employed, and any of the other topics addressed in Chapter 3.

Following such a structured planning process may at first seem awkward, but teachers usually find that if they do so, even going so far as to time themselves so that they complete each step efficiently, they can finish their face-to-face

Figure 6.2
Marilyn's Sixty-Minute Planning Protocol

PRE-MEETING

GE teacher reviews upcoming curriculum for discussion at the meeting

MEETING

TIME ALLOTTED	TOPIC
12 minutes	1. The general education teacher outlines upcoming curriculum and content for material that will be addressed within the context of the class.
10 minutes	2. Both teachers need to review student data. This will help them identify student learning status, gaps in student learning, and specialized student needs that may affect instructional decisions.
15 minutes	3. Both teachers discuss points of difficulty in the upcoming instruction. What are possible barriers to student learning? How could these challenges be lessened or overcome?
15 minutes	4. Both teachers discuss patterns for their co-teaching. They should consider the six co-teaching approaches (and variations), identify patterns in your class of when you review, have assessments, etc., and decide when and where the six approaches fit the best.
8 minutes	5. This time is reserved for partnership discussions, including co-teaching concerns, communication, housekeeping items, and successes/issues related to the past four-week period.

POST-MEETING

SE teacher or the other specialist prepares any specially designed instruction, accommodations or modifications that are student-specific as well as contributing to general strategies for differentiation.

planning session with a strong shared understanding of the instruction to come and the ways they will ensure their diverse students can succeed in learning it.

Strategies to Supplement Face-to-Face Planning

The secret to effective planning for co-teaching is to realize that face-to-face planning should be just a single component of the process. Both electronic planning and planning on-the-spot should accompany the face-to-face collaboration.

Electronic Planning

In the world of business, electronic collaboration is the norm, and lessons learned from that profession have quickly been applied to education, creating innovative ways for teachers to collaborate even when they cannot meet face-to-face.

Wikis. If you are familiar with wikis, you know that they are, in essence, easily editable webpages that users may create and use for a variety of purposes, including on-line collaboration. If you have not used a wiki, one way to think about it is as a shared virtual office in the Internet cloud, a location either one of you can easily access. In your shared "office," you can post documents, revise and re-post them, leave notes for one another, and share instructional materials.

One basic use of a wiki is for posting and expanding lesson plans. That is, the general education teacher does the typical lesson planning that aligns with the required curriculum, following school and district guidelines. Once a week's worth of plans is posted (preferably a full week prior to instructional delivery) and based on the macro planning that has already occurred, the special educator or ESL teacher is able to annotate the basic lesson plans, noting accommodations that are needed, addressing academic vocabulary instruction, and inserting specially designed instructional strategies needed by students with disabilities. With this information posted, both educators have access to the entire instructional package. Further, they are able to post messages to each other within the wiki, and so they may discuss whether a specific idea will work or whether additional adjustments are needed.

The options for co-teaching using a wiki are endless. Teachers may create and revise a rubric for evaluating student work, they may post data related to students' classroom performance, and they may prepare various assessments to determine student mastery of content. Some teachers set up a wiki with folders for assessments, each unit of instruction, a shared calendar, and other instructional components. What is most appealing is that either teacher can access the wiki at any time and from any location — they easily collaborate asynchronously.

Many school districts already subscribe to a wiki platform. If this is the case for you, it should be a simple matter to request a co-teaching wiki for you and your partner or to access the platform and create your group (of two). If you do not have access to a wiki, there are several free options, many designed specifically for teachers. These include

- Wikispaces
- PBWorks
- Wikidot, and
- Google Groups.

The web addresses and brief explanations of the services offered through these sites are provided in the appendix to this chapter.

Social learning platforms (SLPs). The newest generation of education options for collaboration is referred to as *social learning platforms*. If a wiki is like a shared office, a social learning platform is like sharing an entire community. SLPs are designed specifically for teachers and their students. They enable teachers to post course content, facilitate student discussions, receive work from students and post student grades, differentiate assignments among students, conduct student polls, and make homework and grades available for parent viewing. In essence, co-teachers are able, on an SLP, to do everything that is offered on a wiki and more. SLPs also have discussion options that can be made available only to the teachers, and so discussion of student assignments and upcoming plans is easily available.

The best known social learning platform is Edmodo. Another emerging site is Schoology. Like the wiki sites just mentioned, these options are described in more detail in the appendix for this chapter. If you and your students have reasonable Internet access, an SLP may be more attractive than a wiki, but keep in mind that setting up a comprehensive SLP is a significant and time-consuming undertaking. Some professionals report that they gradually build their courses.

E-mail and text messages. Although some teachers plan using e-mail, it generally is considered to be an outdated electronic collaboration strategy. There are several reasons for this view: Most importantly, e-mail is completely linear in the sense that if I send something to you, I have to wait for you to respond before taking further action. Otherwise we are likely to miscommunicate or exchange incorrect versions of whatever documents we are working on. In addition, e-mail tends to get buried in the various folders of an e-mail system. In some cases, capacity limits also lead to e-mail being deleted without notice. Generally, co-teachers spend valuable time trying to find earlier correspondence or searching through folders to locate the attachment sent sometime in the past. Sharing and keeping all items in a single location is a much more efficient and effective system!

Text messages may be an attractive option, but their value for planning is limited by their transitory nature. Teachers should be accountability for their planning. That means that lessons should be prepared, and the specially designed instruction should be embedded within those lessons. The options already discussed permit this to occur, and for the documentation to be preserved. Text messages are fine for quick notes or questions, but they do not create a permanent record and do not comprise an adequate electronic planning process.

A note of caution. Of course, as with any on-line access, a few cautions should be kept in mind. First, you should be sure that school district policy permits teachers to use a wiki or social learning platform that is not on a district server. In addition, you should be sure that if you create a wiki you set it up so that it is private, so that only you and your co-teacher may access it. Third, it may be wise when using any type of cloud computing to use only student initials or a randomly generated numerical code for students so that concerns about privacy and confidentiality are addressed.

Cautions, though, should not prevent you from exploring the powerful alternatives to face-to-face collaboration. By accessing these and similar tools, you will find that you are creating an entirely new culture for co-teaching planning.

Planning on the Spot

If co-teachers create a schedule of macro-planning meetings partnered with electronic planning, and they ensure that both know the key concepts about to be addressed, the instructional dilemmas that students may encounter, and the expectations for projects and activities, they then can fill in details or address problems (for example, teacher absence, being behind schedule, deciding how to address a student behavior issue) with planning on-the-spot. That is, they can quickly touch base about day-to-day teaching matters using brief snippets of time such as these:

Warm-ups. In many classrooms, instruction begins with some type of warm-up activity. Co-teachers can use this time for planning on the fly. At the start of the class period, or in elementary schools when the specialist arrives for co-teaching, the students are directed to complete, independently or possibly with a partner, an appropriate instructional activity. The activity may be a problem similar to the type introduced the day before, it might be a question students are to answer using their textbooks, or it might be a reading or writing assignment. Students are directed to do the activity without interrupting the teachers unless an emergency arises. The three or four minutes for the activity create an opportunity for the co-teachers to touch base to be sure they're ready for the day's lesson.

Review and predict. For elementary students in or secondary classrooms when the specialist comes in for the second half of a block-scheduled class, planning on the fly can be part of the instruction itself. When the special educator or ESL teacher enters the room, one of the two teachers asks students to briefly review what they have been doing and learning. This helps the special educator get oriented to the day's classroom activities. One of the teachers then asks the students to relate the activity that is to occur with both teachers present. Clearly this option implies that the general education teacher has prepared students in advance for co-teaching, but that often will happen just because of scheduling. However, having students stop to review their learning and think about what they've been told will occur next is sound instructional practice and, like instructional warm-ups, helps the specialist prepare for the lesson.

Passing period prepping. Although certainly not ideal, if middle and high school co-teachers have used face-to-face and electronic planning so they both have knowledge of upcoming instruction, some last-minute planning can occur during the minutes between class periods, provided the specialist can get to the classroom before the bell rings. For example, the general education teacher might explain that he would like to continue discussing the similarities between two periods in history while the special education teacher takes small groups of students to the side to fill in the sections of the class timeline on which they have been working. This option permits brief conversations that, based on the more detailed planning, can foster effective teaching and learning.

Instructional videos. If teachers need a bit of extra time to discuss their plans and an appropriate instructional video is available, showing the video can give the teachers a few additional minutes of time to plan. Although the quality of this time is not high because of the need to monitor students, it can occasionally help the teachers find the valuable minutes that will make the teaching and learning more successful.

Although every teacher would like more planning time, the strategies above can provide enough time to make co-teaching feasible and deliberate. For students who are learning English or those with IEPs, this model for planning also ensures that specialists are meeting in a meaningful way their obligation to provide the specialized instruction to which their students are entitled.

Other Logistics

Although the availability of co-planning time is the most often mentioned logistical issue for co-teaching (Walsh, 2012), several other matters must be addressed for co-teaching to be effective and sustainable. However, many of these are administrative issues, and for that reason they are addressed here only selectively and briefly. Those included are class composition and staffing. An in-depth discussion of these topics (as well as others, such as scheduling) is available in the administrator's companion to this teacher's co-teaching manual.

Class Composition

After co-planning time, the most frequently mentioned logistical challenge to co-teaching relates to students. In this section, the most common dilemmas regarding students are considered, including which students with special needs are appropriate candidates for co-teaching, what the overall co-taught class size should be, how many students with disabilities should be in a co-taught class, and who the other students should be. Note, though, that virtually no research exists that provides definitive answers to the questions posed. Instead, state policies, mandates established in court cases, and my own three decades of working with school professionals are the bases for the guidelines offered.

Which students with special needs benefit from co-teaching? If resources were unlimited, co-teaching might benefit nearly every student with a special need. In reality, professionals must sometimes make difficult decisions about the best instructional option for each student. For students with disabilities, in some schools a decision is made to provide co-teaching for those who need "just a little more support" to "push them over" to reaching the goals on annual assessments. Although this is understandable, it seems in many cases that such students really need a strong general education teacher, appropriate accommodations, and support from peers or possibly a paraprofessional. Another approach is to provide co-teaching for students who could not otherwise gain access to the general curriculum. These are students for whom accommodations and a small amount of support are not sufficient; this in many cases is a wise investment of special education resources. Of course, it is the student's IEP team that is responsible for making the decision about student placement in various settings.

For students in ESL programs, little has been written about placement decisions. However, some authors (e.g., Honigsfeld & Dove, 2010) suggest that students who are newcomers or who have almost no English proficiency need at least some service in a separate setting. However, after they have moved beyond that stage, co-teaching should be considered an option for immersion language learning.

How many students with disabilities or other special needs should be in a co-taught class? In some schools, all the students with disabilities at a grade level or in a particular core academic course are grouped in a single section. This tactic undermines the entire purpose of a co-taught class, that is, for students to access the same curriculum alongside their peers without disabilities. Overall, it is recommended that no more than approximately 20 percent (elementary) to 33 percent (high school) of any co-taught class group be students with disabilities. Note, though, that this guideline is an approximation. Other factors, including student behavior problems, student intensity of academic needs, overall class size, and amount of co-teaching service available may affect the number of students with disabilities assigned to a co-taught class.

For English language learners, the above percentage generally is recommended if the overall number of these students in the school is relative low (no more than 15-20 percent). If more ELLs are enrolled, the percentages may need to be a bit higher. If a school has many ELLs, it often is preferable to group them in classes (especially in elementary schools) based on their level of English proficiency. By doing this, the amount of service provided can be appropriately adjusted.

Which other students should be placed in a co-taught class? A foundational premise for co-teaching is that the class group consists of clusters of students with special needs surrounded by a heterogeneous set of typical peers. Sadly, this expectation is often overlooked or deliberately ignored (e.g., Burris, & Welner, 2005). In some elementary schools, struggling readers are not just grouped for core skill instruction (as is recommended in research); they spend the entire language arts block with other struggling readers and have few opportunities to learn from peer models. In middle schools, all the lowest achieving students sometimes are assigned to one team, and then they travel together from class to class, forming, for all intents and purposes, a *de facto* special education segregated class. In high schools, levels of courses may be formed. For example, ninth-grade English may be the standard course, but another course, called Foundations of English, is created to cover more "basic" skills. When students are assigned based on achievement level, a tracked system quickly emerges. Across all grade levels, counselors sometimes say "But there are two of you in there..." as a rationale for assigning every student perceived to have a learning or behavior problems to the co-taught class.

If any of these patterns is common in your school, it is unlikely co-teaching can be sustainable; keeping up the necessary pace for the curriculum becomes nearly impossible. You might try discussing this matter with the person responsible for scheduling since sometimes classes are composed without realizing the problems caused. Alternatively, this is a conversation to have with your principal. What this type of arrangement suggests is that a school is tracking students.

Staffing for Co-Teaching

Teachers and administrators often indicate that co-teaching is not feasible without an allocation of special education teacher or ESL teaching staff beyond what typically is provided in traditional programs (e.g., Russ, Chiang, Rylance, & Bongers, 2001). Sometimes this may be true, especially when special educators are the case managers for 30 or more students or when ESL teachers are responsible for 40 or even more students. However, if caseloads are 25 or fewer students for special educators and 30 or fewer students for ESL teachers, then the conversation often should focus on how much co-teaching should occur, in which subject areas, and how existing staff members can be used most effectively. Although you should check on local policies regarding some of the ideas that follow, these suggestions might help you and your colleagues find ways to make co-teaching seem feasible with existing professional staff. Remember that these ideas might also be mixed and matched to address your specific needs.

- Staffing sometimes is an issue because specialists are accustomed to working only with the students on their caseloads (e.g., I handle all the primary level students and my colleagues serves all those in the intermediate grades). Blending might help. For example, in an elementary school, if two special educators or ESL teachers stagger their schedules so that pullout services can be available for nearly an entire day, then students needing more intensive support can receive it while co-teaching is still a feasible service delivery option (but not all day for all students). However, both teachers — not just one — may serve some students. In high school, teachers should divide co-teaching by subject area, not students. That is, one specialist co-teaches in English (all levels) while another co-teaches in math (all levels). Each will assist in serving the other's students, but co-teaching will be far more likely to occur meaningfully.

- Another alternative is for paraprofessional support to be provided in some classes. For example, in a middle school keyboarding class, a paraprofessional might offer support to students because a co-teacher is not needed. The same might be true for high school vocational or related arts classes.

- Consider other types of support for some situations. In elementary schools, parent volunteers can provide support in classrooms. This clearly is not a special education or ESL service, but if the need is for an extra set of hands then perhaps special education or ESL support is not required. In middle schools located close to the high school or a college, future teacher organizations or student interns might serve a similar role. In high school, a service learning course can be created for students who have completed required coursework. Students enrolling in the course can work as teaching assistants in courses they have previously taken, serving as tutors to some students and generally helping the teacher with the diversity of learners. Other forms of peer tutoring also can provide support when co-teaching might not be necessary (McMaster, Fuchs, & Fuchs, 2006). These options do not constitute the delivery of special services, but they may be adequate for some students in some subject areas, freeing specialists to deliver the specially designed instruction that these and other students require in co-taught and separate classes.

The point of these ideas is to prompt you to think carefully about creative solutions for allocating specialists for co-teaching. That often means thinking beyond the traditional configurations in which services have been provided and drawing on all support services in a school. Of course, the types of services and amounts provided must be accurately reflected on students' IEPs or ESL individual learning plans.

For Further Thought

1. What are your expectations for planning time for co-teaching? Are they realistic? How could the planning model outlined in this chapter be adapted to fit your co-teaching situation?

2. What options exist within your district for electronic collaboration? If none are available, what are district policies regarding accessing wikis and social learning platforms? What professional development is available to teachers to learn about these options?

3. If a parent was concerned about the services being provided to her child, what types of documentation could you share that would demonstrate that the required services for that student are being delivered as part of the co-taught class? How could electronic collaboration support teacher accountability for these services?

4. In Chapter 1 you learned about key concepts, including collaboration and inclusiveness. What do these concepts suggest related to staffing for co-teaching programs? What issues related to teachers' sense of control and beliefs about the way co-teaching should be set up affect their beliefs about staffing?

Taking Action

1. With your grade level, team, department, or colleague work group, identify three strategies for creating planning time that might be feasible. Propose them to your administrator with a rationale for why they could work and how they would enhance co-teaching in your school.

2. Request professional development for your school's co-teachers on the use of electronic options for collaboration. Set up a wiki or social learning platform and commit to experimenting with it for at least four weeks.

3. Review the composition of each current or proposed co-taught class in your school. How many of the students in each are typical learners? Students with disabilities? English learners? Students with other special needs? What adjustments are needed for next semester or next year? How will you propose this issue be addressed? Create a plan with your administrator so that class composition improves.

4. How many students are there in your school who are identified as having disabilities (separate out students whose services are called "speech only")? English language learners? Divide that number by the number of specialists. In doing this activity, care should be taken not to completely exclude teachers who typically work completely in separate settings — whether they also could co-teach for brief periods of time should be examined. What is the teacher-student staffing ratio? What does it tell you about the feasibility of co-teaching?

References

Burris, C.C., & Welner, K.G. (2005). A special section on the achievement gap – Closing the achievement gap by detracking. *Phi Delta Kappan, 86,* 594.

Dieker, L. (2007). *Demystifying secondary inclusion: Powerful schoolwide and classroom strategies.* Port Chester, NY: Dude Publishing.

Dieker, L.A., & Murawski, W.W. (2003). Co-teaching at the secondary level: Unique issues, current trends, and suggestions for success. *High School Journal, 86*(4), 1-13.

Hawbaker, B.W., Balong, M., Buckwalter, S., & Runyon, S. (2001). Building a strong BASE of support for all students through coplanning. *Teaching Exceptional Children, 33*(4), 24-30.

Honigsfeld, A., & Dove, M. G. (2010). *Collaboration and co-teaching: Strategies for English learners.* Thousand Oaks, CA: Corwin.

Kilanowski-Press, L., Foote, C. J., & Rinaldo, V. J. (2010). Inclusion classrooms and teachers: A survey of current practices. *International Journal of Special Education, 25*(3), 43-56.

Kohler-Evans, P. A. (2006). Co-teaching: How to make this marriage work in front of the kids. *Education, 127,* 260-264.

McMaster, K.L., Fuchs, D., & Fuchs, L.S. (2006). Research on peer-assisted learning strategies: The promise and limitations of peer-mediated instruction. *Reading & Writing Quarterly, 22*(1), 5-25.

Pearl, C., Dieker, L. A., & Kirkpatrick, R. M. (2012). A five-year retrospective on the Arkansas Department of Education co-teaching project. *Professional Development in Education, 38,* 571-587.Russ, S., Chiang, B., Rylance, B.J., & Bongers, J. (2001). Caseload in special education: An integration of research findings. *Exceptional Children 67,* 161-172.

Russ, S., Chiang, B., Rylance, B.J., & Bongers, J. (2001). Caseload in special education: An integration of research findings. Exceptional Children 67, 161-172.

Spencer, S.A. (2005). Lynne Cook and June Downing: The practicalities of collaboration in special education service delivery. *Intervention in School and Clinic, 40,* 296-300.

Texas Education Agency. (2011). *Co-teaching-a how-to-guide: Guidelines for co-teaching in Texas.* Austin, TX: Author.

Walsh, J. M. (2012). Co-teaching as a school system strategy for continuous improvement. *Preventing School Failure, 56*(1), 29-36.

Chapter 6 Appendix

The worksheets and other information in this appendix are designed to assist you in effectively using planning time and addressing some of the logistical barriers to co-teaching. They are intended to help school professionals think "outside the box" in order to make co-teaching a realistic service option.

Sample Planning Agenda

Dates of Instruction _____

Teachers/Subject_____

Upcoming curriculum topics/units/lessons
(12 minutes)

Student data summary/discussion
(10 minutes)

Likely instructional challenges/specially designed instructional needs
(15 minutes)

Co-Teaching arrangements and assignments
(15 minutes)

Relationship/Communication/Housekeeping/Logistics
(8 minutes)

Wikis and Social Learning Platforms

Educators are quickly learning that electronic collaboration is efficient and effective, especially as a complement to occasional and intensive face-to-face planning sessions. These are several options for creating a wiki or a establishing a social learning site.

Wikis

Wikispaces.com. Millions of educators and thousands of school districts use Wikispaces as a vehicle for on-line collaboration. Teachers may obtain free Wikispace (districts purchase space), which permits them to organize a co-teaching wiki. They can access this site from any location, as long as an Internet connection is available. One example of the capability of this site is that every draft of every document worked on is saved, and so drafts can be compared.

PBWorks.com. This wiki has fewer users than Wikispaces, but it also offers a free basic version for teachers. It allows you to limit who has access to the wiki, and it saves all draft of documents, identifying who has made changes. For student access, you can add up to 100 student names to the basic account.

Wikidot.com. Another wiki site, Wikidot has many of the same free features for teachers are the other sites, including the capability of embedding photos and video. This wiki also has dozens of applications (called modules) built into the wiki itself, allowing you flexibility to address your specific work situation and preferences.

Groups.google.com. Google Groups is a wiki with the benefit of being easily able to access all the other Google-based tools (e.g., Google docs). This platform was updated in 2012 to make it more streamlined and user friendly. The primary drawback of this site is that you must have a gmail address to use it.

Social Learning Platforms

Edmodo.com. Created in 2008, Edmodo boasts more than 15 million teacher and student users worldwide. Co-teachers use this platform to share lesson plans, created work at different levels for their students, conduct student polls, gather and store data on student achievement, and provide a mechanism for student participation. Co-teachers also can blog with educators from around the world.

Schoology.com. This SLP has many features similar to Edmodo. It also enables you to directly import items from Google docs, and it has a unique organizable lesson plan feature. Schoology also permits threaded discussions. As with other sites, co-teachers also may blog on this platform and connect with educators in other locales.

Co-Teaching Based on Student Needs

This form or an adaptation of it can be used to map out student needs and the types of services which will ensure students achieve their goals. Once completed for each student, professionals can use the information to decide on the amount of co-teaching needed or number of co-taught sections needed as well as the need for other services and instructional settings.

Name	Eligibility[1]	Test Data	Service by Subject						Notes
			English/LA	Math	Science	Social Studies	Related Arts	Other	

[1]Eligibility: Use district eligibility categories (for example, LD,ED, ID, OH); for students in ESL programs this column could designate level of language proficiency

Service by subject:

CON=Consultation
RES=supplemental/support
Other A=_____

CT=Co-Teaching
SCI=Separate core instruction
Other B=_____

Chapter 7
Special Circumstances

Learn from yesterday, live for today, hope for tomorrow.
The important thing is not to stop questioning.
~Albert Einstein

Learner Objectives

1. Analyze the implementation of co-teaching for specialists other than special education teachers, including speech-language therapists, teachers of students who are gifted or talented, ESL educators, and others.

2. Discuss the opportunities and limitations of co-teaching based on unusual scheduling arrangements, including split-block and every-other-day models.

3. Evaluate the use of co-teaching in response to intervention (RTI) and vocational, alterative, or juvenile justice settings as well as in separate special education settings.

4. Explore contemporary practices sometimes inaccurately referred to as co-teaching in order to understand their fundamental differences from this service delivery option.

As co-teaching has evolved, its use has expanded in a number of ways. Professionals across more disciplines are using this model for delivering specialized services, creative approaches are being developed in order to make co-teaching available as many students as possible, and co-teaching is being incorporated into programs and in settings beyond typical general education classrooms. And as sometimes happens when an innovation is rapidly and widely implemented, co-teaching has become a misnomer for several emerging practices that have some similarities to co-teaching but that overall lack several of its defining characteristics. All of these topics are the focus for this chapter. The goal is to provide you and your colleagues with enough information across these special circumstances so that you can analyze the implementation of co-teaching in your school, meaningfully distinguish it from other teacher partnerships, and work to make your program more effective for students as well as more sustainable.

Other Professionals Who Co-Teach

The emphasis in this manual has been on co-teaching that occurs between general educators and special education and ESL teachers. However, they are not the only professionals who deliver services using this model. This section briefly addresses some of the characteristics of and procedures for co-teaching for other professionals, and the appendix includes a worksheet for extending this discussion. This section also concludes with a brief analysis of some of the unique aspects of co-teaching as part of ESL programs, items that have not been mentioned in earlier chapters. Keep in mind that for all of the professional groups cited, there is no intent to suggest that co-teaching should be the only service model. It is one powerful means of educating students, but it is not the only means, and it should be complemented by the array of more traditional service models.

Speech-Language Therapists

Just as special educators and ESL teachers have shifted their specialized instruction from separate locations to general education settings, speech-language therapists — especially those in elementary schools — likewise are gradually embracing this service option. The rationale is that many students' speech and language needs can be effectively addressed within the context of the natural language setting, that is, the typical classroom. Professionals also have noted that co-teaching can (a) facilitate sharing of materials, (b) extend services because of modeling by the speech-language therapist, (c) contribute to reducing problems in scheduling services without removing students during core instruction, and (d) embed speech and language skills within that core instruction. Further, at least several studies have found that co-teaching as a delivery mechanism for speech and language services is at least effective and often more effective than instruction in a separate setting (Merritt, 2007).

Types of co-teaching for therapists. Two types of co-teaching have evolved for speech-language therapists (Vicker, 2009). The first and most basic type is sometimes referred to as a push-in model. That is, the therapist regularly goes into the general education classroom, but the two educators do not complete detailed planning or prioritize blending their work with students. The therapist is likely to pull students to the side, possibly including in the group other students known to have difficulties who thus receive incidental benefit. As part of the in-class therapy session, the specialist uses as much as possible the academic vocabulary students are learning, the discussion questions related to the literature or unit of study, or the materials that other students are accessing.

The second approach is called integrated services (Vicker, 2009). This approach calls for the therapist to be much more of a true collaborator in the classroom, building a close partnership with teachers, participating in planning, embedding speech and language services within the context of the general curriculum, and assuming a collegial role during co-teaching time periods. The goal is for students to more readily generalize the speech and language skills they are learning by incorporating them within instruction in the natural learning setting (Bauer, Iyer, Boon, & Fore, 2010). With this type of co-teaching, the partners are more likely to use an array of the co-teaching approaches presented in Chapter 4.

Challenges. Many speech-language therapists believe that co-teaching should be an important part of their professional roles, and the American Speech-Language-Hearing Association (1996) has published a policy statement that endorses inclusive practices, including integrated services, as one option for the delivery of speech and language services. However, the reality in many school districts makes this version of co-teaching extraordinarily difficult to implement. First, many speech-language therapists have high caseloads. If their students are not clustered into a small number of classrooms, they may not be able to provide services appropriately without pulling students from several classes to a separate location. Second, speech-language therapists often work with students in more than one school. Being itinerant compounds immeasurably the scheduling complexity for co-teaching. That is, therapists are trying to complete the services they are required by law to provide while juggling lost time to travel, two or more school schedules, teacher preferences, and so on and so on. In addition, therapists also are faced with the challenge of making decisions about students who need services in a separate setting versus those who would benefit from co-teaching. For example, some students are too distracted in the general education setting to focus on the instruction from the therapist, and for others, the nature of the services they need would be embarrassing or too intrusive in the typical classroom. When all these factors — and sometime others — are part of the situation, speech-language therapists may not be able to co-teach at all, or they may co-teach just in kindergarten and possibly first grade classrooms.

Gifted/Talented Teachers

Another group of professionals sometimes encouraged to co-teach are teachers for students who are gifted and talented (G/T). Of course, the purpose for this co-teaching is somewhat different from that of most other professionals: Rather than focusing on reducing the achievement gap among student groups, its goal is to foster talent development in students so that they accomplish extraordinary achievement, academically or in other areas. The rationale for this service model is straightforward (Hughes & Murawski, 2001): In many locales, resources to deliver gifted/talented services are very limited. Through co-teaching, identified students can receive differentiated instruction while students who profit from this instructional enhancement but who may not be eligible for it receive incidental benefit. Further, by embedding this instruction in the general education class, teachers often are able to continue the enrichment or alternative instruction after the co-teacher leaves. Little research has been completed on co-teaching for students who are gifted/talented, but some authors do report that it can be an effective service model (e.g., Masso, 2004) and some respected professionals in the field support its use (e.g., Van Tassel Baska, 1998).

Types of co-teaching for G/T teachers. Teachers in the gifted/talented field may co-teach using any of the basic approaches and variations of them. However, their co-teaching sometimes is unit-based, that is, occurring only for a specified topic of instruction or for a limited period of time. In other cases, it may be an ongoing arrangement, as occurs in elementary schools when students identified as talented are grouped into a single grade level class, and co-teaching becomes their sole access to the service. In high schools, this type of co-teaching is less common because other options exist for students who are talented, including honors, dual enrollment, and advanced placement courses. In fact, it occasionally happens that co-teaching in advanced high school classes is implemented because students with disabilities are enrolled in them. In those instances, a decision is made that a special educator should partner in the class, and traditional co-teaching is implemented.

Challenges. Co-teaching for teachers of students who are gifted and talented is by no means widespread. It is constrained by several factors. First, because no federal law requires that all states and school districts offer special services to this student group, in many school districts there is no gifted/talented program at all. In other locales, professionals focus these services on just a few students who, especially at the elementary level, may spend part of each day or specified amounts of time each week in a separate setting with peers who are likewise identified as talented. G/T professionals also may have so many responsibilities that their options for co-teaching are limited: They may manage the district's assessment and identification processes, may be responsible for providing professional development on this topic to general education colleagues, and may have to work with students in two or more schools. Finally, there exists in some places a belief that students who are gifted and talented are entitled to instruction that is so significantly different from what is offered in the general education classroom that it cannot and should not be provided through extensive differentiation or alternative activities delivered there.

Reading Specialists

Another school professional who may co-teach, most often in elementary schools, is a reading specialist. This type of co-teaching may involve students designated to receive Title I reading interventions, or it may be part of an all-school initiative to improve reading outcomes for students. The goal is to intensify reading instruction and remediate students' skill deficits while avoiding the problem of removing students from the general education classroom during core academic instruction. In some schools, reading specialists' in-class efforts are focused in the primary grades; in others, they co-teach across grade levels. Most reports of this type of co-teaching are anecdotal; few data are available regarding its impact on student outcomes (e.g., Shaw, 2009).

Types of co-teaching for reading specialists. Two types of co-teaching are typical for reading specialists. If co-teaching is the primary mechanism through which reading support is provided to students, the specialist may co-teach daily in certain classes and grade levels, and the model is very similar to that used for students with disabilities, except that the time allotment often is quite brief, possibly 30 minutes in each class. Alternatively, co-teaching is employed as part of a coaching model. In this approach, the reading specialist may work with the general educator for longer instructional segments (e.g., 45 minutes or an hour), but only for a relatively brief overall period of time (e.g., 2 or 3 weeks). The goal in this approach is for the specialist to model strategies and techniques that the general educator should then continue implementing after co-teaching has concluded.

Challenges. Reading specialists face many of the same challenges as other professionals who co-teach in several classes. They may have high caseloads, and they may struggle to adequately deliver their services across classes because of complexities related to scheduling. In addition, these professionals sometimes also have extensive other responsibilities, such as managing the collection, interpretation, and decision making related to student data; providing professional development to teachers; selecting reading materials for all students; offering highly specialized reading programs that must be delivered in a separate setting; or coordinating the school's intervention process (Jones, Barksdale, Triplett, Potts, Lalik, & Smith, 2010). With each added responsibility, time available for co-teaching decreases. Finally, reading specialists in middle and high schools may spend most of their time delivering reading instruction in separate remedial reading courses.

Library/Media Specialists

The professionals mentioned thus far as potential co-teachers are those who ensure that students with a range of special needs access specialized instruction. However, co-teaching is also being implemented by specialists whose expertise positively affects all students' learning. Library/media specialists are in this group. The goal of this type of co-teaching generally is to embed literature into the core academic instruction occurring in the general education setting, doing so by drawing on the literature and related expertise of the library/media specialist and partnering for instructional delivery. This co-teaching option is intuitively appealing, but accounts of its implementation rely heavily on anecdotal information and recommendations from practitioners rather than research (e.g., Moreillon, 2009).

Types of co-teaching for library/media specialists. The co-teaching of library/media specialists can best be termed episodic. These professionals partner with a teacher for a specific purpose, and when that purpose has been accomplished the co-teaching ends. Thus, the general educators and library/media specialist may partner for one or two weeks while students are completing an interdisciplinary unit on a particular topic. During implementation, the library/media specialist sometimes participates in the class in much the same ways as a special education or ESL teacher, but it is more common that this individual takes the lead during instruction, in some cases functioning as a guest speaker for the class. This option is especially common when the specialist's role is mostly collaboration outside the classroom, that is, meeting with teachers to help them identify and select appropriate literature and other learning resources for the instruction at hand.

Challenges. Although co-teaching involving library/media specialists has tremendous potential, especially as professionals work to implement the Common Core State Standards, it is not in any legislative or legal way mandated, and so whether it exists relies largely on district culture and policies. In addition, this role for library/media specialists must have strong site-based administrator support (Cooper & Bray, 2011). If not, it is likely that the schedule established for them will preclude co-teaching as a feasible option (for example, class groups assigned to come to the library/media center nearly all day, or a schedule of open times when the specialist must be available in case class groups or individual students wish to access the library/media center). Further, even if permitted, unless library/media specialists actively seek colleagues with whom to collaborate, it is not likely this service option will be integral to a school's instructional approaches.

ESL Teachers

Many aspects of co-teaching for ESL teachers are virtually identical to those for special educators, a point that has been emphasized throughout this manual (Dove & Honigsfeld, 2010; Honigsfeld & Dove, 2010). However, these professionals sometimes face challenges somewhat different from those special educators encounter, and those challenges should be noted (e.g., Pawan & Ortloff, 2011).

A beginning point for some ESL teachers is ensuring that all the teachers with whom they work have a reasonable understanding of the goals of an ESL program and students who are English language learners. If your school's ESL program is well-established, this topic may not be an issue. In some schools, though, ESL services are viewed as primarily remedial; in others, they are conceptualized as language instruction that must be completed as a prerequisite to participating in general education classes. In other locales, general education teachers may admit that they know little about the details of what ESL programs do or how their goals are accomplished.

A closely related issue concerns understanding the job responsibilities of ESL teachers and the crucial role of collaboration for classroom partnerships (Gladman, 2012). It is unfortunate — and completely inappropriate — for ESL teachers to function primarily as teaching assistants in classes that are supposed to be co-taught. This is most likely to occur when the general educator believes the most important role for the ESL teacher is providing translation support to the English language learners in the class, and the ESL teacher is uncomfortable directly addressing this topic of classroom roles, of challenging the general educator's understanding of co-teaching. This situation sometimes also has a much broader underlying basis: In some schools, ESL teachers still report that they are not perceived as having knowledge and skills equivalent to those of other teachers and that they sometimes feel like "second class citizens" in their schools and sense bias and devaluing of their contributions. Such a perception may originate in a few teachers' fear or uncertainty, or it may stem from cultural differences between the teachers or between the general educator and ELLs. This problem is most likely to occur in school in which ESL services are relatively new or still needed by only a few students. This climate undermines a collaborative culture and if not addressed can severely limit co-teaching effectiveness.

A third set of co-teaching challenges for ESL teachers concerns the very nature of ESL services and the logistics that are part of ESL programs. For example, a number of models for providing language instruction to students who do not speak English are available, and sometimes decisions have to be made about whether co-teaching can be integrated into the models being implemented. In addition, ESL teachers may have to divide their time across several schools if the number of students needing services is low, and needs may change across the school year, depending on student progress and enrollment changes. Further, because ESL teachers often have many students on their caseloads, they may have to make choices about the number of classrooms in which co-teaching can be justified. Finally, many of the recommendations made in this manual are based on the fact that services for students with disabilities are highly regulated and many practices are the result of litigation that has clarified what must occur. The same is not true for students who are English language learners. When I work with these educators, they sometimes comment on this difference because it leaves them without much-needed clarity when justifying the rationale for and implementing co-teaching.

In thinking about the many challenges ESL teachers encounter in co-teaching programs, it is evident that communication and collaboration is the key. Perhaps even more so than when special educators co-teach, it is imperative that ESL teachers and their general education partners complete relationship-building activities such as those presented in Chapter 3 and establish clear mechanisms for discussing successes and barriers in their co-taught classes.

Other Professionals

Before leaving the topic of specialists who may co-teach, brief mention should be made of several additional professionals. For example, in a few schools adaptive physical educators may co-teach with physical education teachers or with general education teachers. Other professionals may co-teach periodically and for a specific purpose, including counselors and school psychologists. A few other related services providers may embed their services by co-teaching as well, including occupational or physical therapists. Finally, consultants with highly specialized knowledge (e.g., skills for working with students with autism) may co-teach as a means of demonstrating techniques to better reach specific students.

Other professionals not associated with special education or other special services likewise occasionally co-teach. One example is an instructional coach or a behavior management specialist who partners in the classroom for the purpose of assisting the general education teacher to refine instructional practice or improve classroom management. Similarly, social workers or counselors may partner with general educators for specific instructional purposes, as might happen in a school focusing on social and emotional learning (SEL).

Finally, separate mention should be made of itinerant professionals and co-teaching. Sometimes these are specialists already discussed in this section (for example, an ESL teacher in a small district with just a handful of English language learners or a speech-language therapist assigned to three elementary schools). But they also may be specialists who work with students who are blind or low-vision or deaf or hard of hearing, as well as others. These professionals' roles usually are based on consultation, that is, meeting with teachers away from the classroom, completing observations of students, providing to teachers and students needed instructional information and materials, and monitoring student progress. They also usually provide some direct service to the students on their caseloads. Co-teaching is often rare for these professionals because of the complexity of their schedules and the time required to travel from place to place. However, some educators in these roles co-teach for brief periods, especially if they have a student whose IEP indicates this service option or if several students with similar needs are placed in a single classroom.

Unique Co-Teaching Schedules

In some schools, co-teaching is implemented primarily for students with disabilities, those who are English language learners, or others, but somewhat atypical scheduling patterns are used. This sometimes occurs because of decisions about the amount of service needed by students, but at times it is a response to a perceived shortage of professionals to deliver that service. In this section, a few variations of co-teaching based on schedule are briefly discussed.

Full-Day or Half-Day Co-Teaching

A decade ago, it was common in some parts of the U.S. to place several students with relatively significant disabilities in a general education elementary classroom with both a general education and a special education teacher assigned to the class full time, and the overall class size capped so that it was no higher (or even a bit lower) than other class sections in the same grade level. The teachers in these classes functioned as a completely integrated instructional team. Because they had identical schedules, problems related to collaborative planning did not exist, and because they were together for all instruction, issues related to parity, power, trust, and respect were rare. For a small part of the day as needed, the special educator might work with students with disabilities in a separate setting, but the home base for both the students and teacher was clearly the general education classroom.

This model has largely disappeared, but in a few school districts it is still considered the preferred structure for a co-teaching program. The logic is that if students have disabilities, they need support throughout the school day, not just for a period of time during language arts or math instruction, particularly if their disabilities are significant enough that they otherwise would be assigned to a separate setting for much of the school day.

Two variations of a full-time co-teaching program occasionally are used. In a few high schools and especially for core academic courses such as 9th grade English and U.S. History, a general education and a special education teacher will be partnered to co-teach the course for the entire day, thus working with all the students with disabilities who are taking the course. At the elementary level, a variation occurs in which a special educator splits the day between two general education classes, half of the day in each. For the half of the day when the special educator is not present, a paraprofessional is assigned. In this variation, the classroom with students with disabilities always has two adults present, either two teachers or a teacher and a paraprofessional.

If you plan to co-teach or currently are co-teaching in a model such as these, you have exceptional opportunities for collaboration seldom available to other co-teachers. One caution about this type of co-teaching is that too much assistance may be available in the classroom, especially at the elementary level. Professionals may have to take care that students are encouraged to develop skills for independent learning rather than relying unnecessarily on the fact that two teachers are available to provide assistance.

Split Class Co-Teaching

In middle and high schools, most often when block scheduling has created class periods of 70-90 minutes, co-teaching may be split in one of two ways. First, a single special educator or ESL teacher may be expected to spend half of a single period in one class and then spend the other half in a different class. Although not preferred, this type of schedule can be a viable option. However, details must be carefully considered. First, professionals must be certain that students' instructional needs can be met using this approach, including the required minutes of special education service for students with disabilities. A companion consideration is whether this model should be limited to only certain situations, for example, used in 11th or 12th grade English classes (after high stakes testing is completed) but not in 9th grade English. Yet another consideration concerns flexibility: This approach is more palatable if the three teachers involved can negotiate about when the co-teaching occurs. For a week with particularly difficult material, the specialist might begin the class period every day co-teaching in that class first, but the following week the order would be reversed. Another option would be to spend the entire class period in one setting for three days, but then to do the same for the other class for the following three days. Of course, conversations about flexible co-teaching arrangements should have administrative approval and also must meet students' needs.

A different type of co-teaching split sometimes occurs in middle and high schools in relation to teachers' status as being highly qualified in core academic content areas. In these situations, co-teaching occurs for the first part of the instructional period. Once all initial instruction is completed, the specialist leaves the class with the designated students to provide re-teaching, remediation, or other instruction.

This model may be necessary, but several serious risks also exist. First, even if teachers agree that initial instruction has concluded, if a student in the general education setting asks a question that the teacher answers for all the students, the students who have left the room have, in essence, still missed out. Further, for students with disabilities, this structure must be included on the IEP; if students are supposed to be in a general education setting but are daily spending half of the time in a separate setting, a violation of their rights may be occurring. Finally, the potentially stigmatizing impact of this model on students must be weighed, especially in middle school and 9th grade. Some students may be so embarrassed that they refuse to leave, and the situation may easily escalate to a serious behavior incident.

Every-Other-Day Co-Teaching

I routinely hear from middle and high school co-teachers that, because of problems related to schedule and the number of specialists available to co-teach, their co-teaching occurs every other day, even when the class meets daily. This is a last-resort co-teaching option that usually results in frustration for teachers and limited benefit for students. Its primary problem is that the specialist working in the general education class has never been there the day before, and so never can be sure what was accomplished through the preceding day's instruction, which students understood (or didn't understand) the instruction, and how the instruction should be adjusted for that day. Instead of this approach, professionals should meet with administrators to find an alternative, perhaps co-teaching for two days in one class and three in the other, alternating the arrangement across weeks. Alternatively, perhaps a unit-based approach could work in which co-teaching occurs daily for a week or more during particularly crucial or challenging instruction, and then it occurs in the other class for a comparable period of time.

Programs and Settings

In addition to various professionals implementing co-teaching and a wide range of scheduling options, consideration should be given to several specific programs that are using this option for meeting student needs. Three relatively common examples are the use of co-teaching as a strategy in (a) response-to-intervention (RTI), multi-tiered systems of support (MTSS), or other remedial programs; (b) vocational, alternative, or juvenile justice settings; and (c) special education classrooms, whether in typical schools or separate schools.

Co-Teaching as a Remedial Intervention

Class groups that are co-taught typically have a disproportionately higher than average number of learners with special needs. After all, the recommendation is to place clusters of such students in the classes so that specially designed instruction can be efficiently and effectively delivered. Not surprisingly, administrators and counselors or schedulers sometimes use this fact as a basis for assigning additional students with special needs to co-taught class sections. The effect is that the overall class composition does not reflect a diversity of student abilities but instead includes mostly students who struggle with learning or have behavior problems. This practice is not recommended because co-teaching is premised on surrounding the learners with special needs with a heterogeneous mix of classmates, as noted in Chapter 6. Without diversity of ability and achievement in the class group, outcomes for students who struggle are unlikely to significantly improve.

This perspective on the student members of a co-taught class should be kept in mind when co-teaching is proposed as a means of providing general remedial education services. For example, in RTI or MTSS models, professionals may decide that all students who need Tier 2 instruction (that is, intensive instruction to address an identified achievement gap) should be grouped in a single classroom and co-teaching employed as a strategy for increasing the instructional intensity of the class. At the elementary school level, if this approach is used for highly focused skill instruction for relatively brief periods of time (30-50 minutes per day, depending on the age and grade levels of the students), it may serve a valuable purpose (Murawski & Hughes, 2009). A special educator or ESL teacher may be able to provided needed services, and other students may also be beneficiaries of their expertise. However, if students are grouped for the entire day by reading skill level, as sometimes happens when a decision is made that this approach would make scheduling services easier, then the requirement of heterogeneity is lost, and student success is much less likely. Further, this type of approach is likely to result in a high rate of teacher burnout as professionals struggle daily to address all the complex needs of all their students.

At the middle and high school level, an example is found when remedial reading classes are offered. Whether these are part of an RTI or MTSS model, or just an option for students who are significantly below grade level in reading, the same type of analysis is appropriate. Co-teaching in such classes can create an opportunity for students to receive highly individualized reading instruction that may help them significantly reduce the gap between their achievement and that of their peers. However, in some cases — especially in smaller schools — being grouped for this type of reading class results in the students being grouped together across all their core academic classes. The result is a tracked model of education, one that is likely to result in disappointing student outcomes.

This discussion illustrates that co-teaching can be a valuable option for students with disabilities and other special needs. It often is employed as part of Tier 1 instruction. That is, it is part of the high quality and evidence-based practices that all students should receive, including those students with special needs. Implemented carefully with close attention to the impact on the rest of students' instructional schedules, it also can be a means of intensifying instruction for struggling learners. However, this use of co-teaching also includes risks that low-achieving students will, in essence, be ability grouped for the entire school day.

Vocational, Alternative, or Juvenile Justice Settings

Although most professionals work in the elementary, middle, or high schools that serve the students of their community or catchment area, many specialized schools also are part of the education system. Their unique characteristics sometimes lead to questions about co-teaching options and concerns about co-teaching feasibility.

One issue that may arise concerns the mix of students in the classes. In some vocational, alternative, or juvenile justice settings, a majority (or, sometimes, all) of the students have special needs. When taught by a general educator and a special educator, these classes fall into the same category as the hybrid model described in the next section. That is, the number of students with disabilities is higher than generally recommended for co-teaching, but the professionals bring to the class the different types of expertise that make this model effective.

A second concern for alternative and juvenile justice settings relates to student transience. Students may attend such a school for as little as a month or as much as a school year or more. Teachers sometimes explain that when their goal is to help students keep up with the curriculum at their own school, nearly all class activity is individualized, and the co-teaching approaches are not particularly applicable. This is understandable. Co-teaching may occur, but it is likely that it will entail primarily teaming (as both adults work with students individually) or alternative teaching (as a small group with similar tasks works with one of the educators).

In vocational settings, questions sometimes arise about the role that a special educator should play in the classroom. Particularly in a vocation class in which particular expertise is needed to operate equipment, general educators understandably may be reluctant to share instructional responsibility. This dilemma usually can be overcome with careful conversations about the plan for the instruction and appropriate roles and responsibilities for both professionals.

A final matter that sometimes arises regarding vocational, alternative, and juvenile justice settings involves guidelines that prevent co-teaching. In some cases, special education services are only considered provided if they occur in a location other than the classroom. In other situations, institutional policies dictate whether or not co-teaching is even a permitted option. In yet others, special educators must be available for crisis situations in both the classroom and the school, and so co-teaching is not employed as a service option because it is often interrupted.

Multiple Professionals in a Special Education Setting

Educators sometimes explain that they are co-teaching but they are in a unique situation. They then describe an option such as one of these:

- A general education teacher is assigned to teach a group of students with disabilities in a high school special education setting with the special educator as a teaching partner. This assignment is made because of the combination of student needs (often related to behavior) and the core subject highly-qualified status of the special educator.

- A speech-language therapist provides therapy services twice each week in the middle school separate special education classroom for students with significant intellectual disabilities.

- Two special educators responsible for students with significant needs who are in separate classes blend their groups and share instruction for science and vocational activities.

The first two examples, although they are not typical arrangements, they approximate the criteria for co-teaching. The professionals delivering instruction have different types of expertise, and by blending their skills they can create instruction that is significantly more intense and more responsive to their diverse learners' needs. However, both of these examples violate the premise that the student group should be heterogeneous. When viewed in totality, they are hybrid examples of co-teaching, matching the core model in some ways but not in others. When students' needs are so high that participation in a classroom with typical peers is not possible, these options are reasonable means to provide a seamless and high equality education to students.

The third example is not co-teaching, and probably would more correctly be included in the next section. When two special educators partner, they bring similar knowledge and skills to teaching, and they are likely to share similar views about essential aspects of the teaching/learning process. Their practice is more appropriately called team teaching. It may be a highly valuable way to work with the students; it just is not co-teaching in the sense and with the expectations outlined through this manual.

Not Exactly Co-Teaching

It sometimes seems in education as though we find a term that we like, and then it is over-used until its meaning is lost and its practice is diluted. Co-teaching currently runs that risk. If you recall the information from Chapter 1, co-teaching has very specific elements and characteristics, and its effective practice is based on those qualities. Unfortunately, several other programs and instructional arrangements are gradually being placed under the umbrella of co-teaching, even though this is an inaccurate understanding. Three examples are provided here to illustrate the problem, and the appendix includes a set of questions for further distinguishing co-teaching from similar but distinctly different practices.

Interdisciplinary Teams for Common Core Instruction

As professionals across the country apply the Common Core State Standards in their instruction, they sometimes are experimenting with new models for content delivery. At the elementary level, for example, science or social studies content may be integrated into the language arts program through the selection of literature and prioritized discussions and activities. This type of integration may be completed in solo-taught as well as co-taught classes, and there are no direct implications for the understanding of co-teaching. However, in high schools, one response to the emphasis on interdisciplinary studies is to blend disparate courses, including the content and the groups of students assigned to each.

Course combinations vary considerably. Many examples of social studies courses being combined with English courses can be found. However, English courses also are being combined with science courses (for example, Life Science), with an emphasis on predicting and problem solving, reading of expository text, and persuasive writing based on observations. Another combination is physical education with anatomy and physiology, in which precise understanding of the components and functions of the human body are blended with their implementation through physical activity.

In some locales, these interdisciplinary courses are being referred to as co-teaching. However, they are more accurately termed team teaching, because they are consistent with the many examples and long history of that practice. They do not have the characteristics of co-teaching that make it unique, including a lower teacher-student ratio, specialist expertise, and the delivery of specially designed instruction. It seems that as such models emerge, it will be important to more fully understand them, to complete research related to their impact on student outcomes, and to explore how the professional relationships that exist in such courses are similar to and different from those in co-taught classes.

Schedule Filling

In contrast to most educators who have teaching schedules that are full and limited time to prepare for lessons or to collaborate, in a few school districts there are teachers in middle and especially in high schools who, because of the combination of their specific licensure status, the demand for particular courses, and the vagaries of scheduling, do not have full teaching loads. Understandably, administrators have considered how to handle situations in which a teacher has a free period, that is, is not scheduled to teach a class but already has designated planning and lunch periods.

One solution has been to assign these teachers to assist in a solo-taught class that has several students with disabilities or other special needs. The logic is that the instructor of that class would value the extra help, given the diversity of the student group. This arrangement sometimes is called co-teaching, but it is not. First, the second professional was assigned completely on the basis of schedule and availability; it is not a deliberate arrangement blending different types of expertise. Second, no specialized instruction is being delivered. That is, the second professional is present to simply provide support, not to ensure students receive special education or ESL services. Third, it is difficult to even consider such arrangements team teaching, because the second professional is not assigned in order to integrate curriculum or contribute to the planning and delivery of initial instruction. In fact, the second professional may have little connection to the course assigned, as occurred for the fine arts teacher assigned to partner with an Algebra II teacher. No expectation existed that the former teacher would contribute to the primary instruction.

Small-Group Reading Instruction

As professionals work to improve the academic achievement outcomes of students with a variety of special needs, one strategy increasingly used is to find ways to intensify instruction by placing more adults in the general education classroom during reading instruction. Thus, in a single room, there may be a general educator, a special educator, a reading specialist, and a speech-language therapist, all working with students in groups that have been established based on students' skill levels and needs. Often these groups are durable. That is, each professional works daily with the same students for the allocated "co-teaching time," and the specialists typically are instructing the students with the greatest needs. Students who progress quickly may be moved to a different group, and overall group assignments may be reviewed and adjusted monthly or quarterly.

Grouping by skills may be part of co-teaching, but when the arrangement just described (or a similar one) is the only approach implemented, it is more a strategy for group size reduction than for classroom partnership. It's not that this is wrong or inappropriate, it's that the professionals could just as easily be working in separate locations because the instruction is not integrated, especially when the specialists are working with "their" students (that is, the special educator is teaching students with disabilities while the speech-language therapist instructs students on his caseload and the reading specialist supports students on her roster).

Student Teaching

As changes have occurred in preservice teacher preparation over the past several years, dissatisfaction has been expressed about traditional student teaching. In these models and regardless of grade level, teacher candidates begin a semester-long fulltime field experience by observing their cooperating teacher, and they gradually assume increased responsibility for instruction. Eventually, the teacher candidate is expected to complete all of the master teacher's responsibilities, including planning for instruction, teaching, and assessing student progress. In many programs, the cooperating teacher is expected, for several weeks, to largely withdraw from the classroom. Critics have noted that this student teaching approach slows down the induction of the teacher candidate, de-emphasizes collaboration between the veteran and the novice, and artificially removes the expertise of the master teacher from the classroom.

Recently, an alternative structure has been proposed for student teaching, and it is being implemented at some universities. In this approach, collaboration between the teacher candidate and master teacher is highlighted, and the educators "co-teach," working in partnership and implementing the approaches much as described in Chapter 4 (Darragh, Picanco, Tully, & Henning, 2011). They may parallel teach, simultaneously facilitating student discussions; station teach, with one teacher delivering new instruction while the other facilitates a problem solving session; or utilize one teach, one observe, with either professional gathering data on student behavior or other variables.

Without intending to in any way evaluate this alternative student teaching model, it is important to recognize that although approaches that are part of co-teaching are employed and the model is called co-teaching, it does not meet generally accepted criteria for this service delivery option. First, the novice-veteran partnerships, by their very nature, are not based on parity. One teacher is a beginner who is gaining experience and learning from the other, a master teacher who eventually provides an assessment of the novice's readiness to complete the teacher preparation program. Thus, there is a fundamental and appropriate difference in power between them. In contrast, co-teaching is premised on parity, a relationship is which power is essentially equal.

A second key difference concerns the purpose of the arrangement. In co-teaching, the goal is the delivery of specialized instruction of some sort, and its power is based on the differences in expertise of the teachers. However, in the student teaching model, a novice teacher is placed with a veteran with the same (albeit advanced) area of expertise. The goal is not the provision of specialized instruction, nor is it the deliberate increase in instructional intensity that is a hallmark of co-teaching.

For Further Thought

1. Who are the professionals who co-teach at your school or district? If some professionals work in classrooms and others pull students or otherwise work in separate settings, what does this say about a seamless education for students? What ideas do you have about your own co-teaching program and the potential involvement of other professionals?

2. Are any of the unusual co-teaching scheduling options in place in your school? What is the history of this approach? What is the rationale? What are the advantages and disadvantages of the approach being used?

3. Should co-teaching occur in specialized settings such as vocational or alternative schools, juvenile justice settings, and even separate special education classrooms? Why or why not? What factors do you think should be taken into account?

4. Why does it matter that some education practices are called co-teaching when they do not meet the criteria for this service delivery model? How does the information about practices that are not co-teaching but sometimes called by that term affect your school and district?

Taking Action

1. If your school is implementing any of the practices described in this chapter, construct a chart. On one side make a list of the essential elements of co-teaching. On the other describe how your co-teaching included (or does not include) each element. Use the chart as the basis for a conversation about refining co-teaching practices in your school.

2. Ask professionals in your school — other than general educator — to speak briefly at a staff, team, or department meeting about their professional

preparation, key roles, and range of responsibilities. You could do this as a game, asking them to prepare statements and having the rest of the staff mark each as true or false.

3. If co-teaching at your school involves only special education, poll staff members, administrators, and parents about their perception of using this approach for other services available at your school. Analyze your results, and use them to discuss future directions for co-teaching across programs.

4. If your co-teaching involves any of the scheduling variations noted in this chapter, use the chart in the appendix to make a list of the advantages and disadvantages of it. Outline other possible options, and make a similar list. Then involve key stakeholders in deciding whether any changes should be put in place for the next school year.

References

American Speech-Language-Hearing Association. (1996). *Inclusive practices for children and youths with communication disorders* [position statement]. Retrieved from www.asha.org/policy.

Bauer, K. L., Iyer, S., Boon, R. T., & Fore, C. (2010). 20 ways for classroom teachers to collaborate with speech-language pathologists. *Intervention in School and Clinic, 45*, 333-337.

Cooper, O. P., & Bray, M. (2011). School library media specialist-teacher collaboration: Characteristics, challenges, opportunities. *Techtrends: Linking Research and Practice to Improve Learning, 55*(4), 48-55.

Darragh, J. J., Picanco, K. E., Tully, D., & Henning, A. (2011). "When teachers collaborate, good things happen": Teacher candidate perspectives of the co-teach model for the student teaching internship. *AILACTE Journal, 8*, 83-104.

Dove, M., & Honigsfeld, A. (2010). ESL coteaching and collaboration: Opportunities to develop teacher leadership and enhance student learning. *TESOL Journal, 1*(1), 3-22.

Gladman, A. (2012). Collaborative interdisciplinary team teaching: A model for good practice. In A. Honigsfeld & M. G. Dove (Ed.), *Coteaching and other collaborative practices in the EFL/ESL classroom: Rationale, research, reflections, and recommendations* (pp. 49-58). Charlotte, NC: Information Age Publishing.

Honigsfeld , A., & Dove, M. (2010, Spring). Co-teaching: 201---How to support ELLs. *New Teacher Advocate*, pp. 4-5.

Hughes, C. E., & Murawski, W. A. (2001). Lessons from another field: Applying coteaching strategies to gifted education. *Gifted Child Quarterly, 45*, 195-204.

Jones, T., Barksdale, M. A., Triplett, C. F., Potts, A., Lalik, R., & Smith, C. (2010). Complexities in the roles of reading specialists. *International Journal of Education, 2*(2), 1-21. Retrieved from http://www.macrothink.org/journal/index.php/ije/article/view/515.

Masso, G. (2004, Summer). Co-teaching in a differentiated classroom: The impacts on third grade gifted and talented math students [newsletter]. *National Research Center on the Gifted and Talented*. Retrieved January 8, 2013 from http://www.gifted.uconn.edu/nrcgt/newsletter/summer04/sumer044.html.

Merritt, D. D. (2007, January). *Research summaries on SLP co-teaching*. Middletown, CT: State Education Resource Center. Retrieved from http://ctserc.org/isss/Research%20Summaries%20-%20SLPs%20as%20Co-teachers.pdf?2fa6f942252db2ec6c621fe255459617=gqruqgyj.

Moreillon, J. (2009). Reading and the library program: An expanded role for 21st-century SLMS. *Knowledge Quest, 38*(2), 24-31.

Murawski, W. W., & Hughes, C. E. (2009). Response to intervention, collaboration, and co-teaching: A logical combination for successful systemic change. *Preventing School Failure, 53,* 267-277.

Pawan, F., & Ortloff, J. H. (2011). Sustaining collaboration: English-as-a-second-language, and content-area teachers. *Teaching and Teacher Education, 27,* 463-471.

Shaw, M. E. (2009). Teaching and empowering reading specialists to be literacy coaches: Vision, passion, communication and collaboration. *NERA Journal, 45*(1), 7-18.

Van Tassel-Baska, J. (1998). *Excellence in educating the gifted.* Denver, CO: Love.

Vicker, Beverly. (2009). The 21st century speech language pathologist and integrated services in classrooms. *The Reporter, 14*(2), 1-5, 17.

Chapter 7 Appendix

The information in this chapter may pertain to your co-teaching, or it may not be relevant, and the same is true for the activities included in this appendix. It includes activities to assist you in analyzing co-teaching options across professional roles, practices that may or may not meet the criteria to be named co-teaching, and scheduling practices and their advantages and disadvantages.

Co-Teaching Across Professional Roles

A key to effective co-teaching is understanding each other's professional roles and responsibilities. The chart below can be used by partners, or it can be used for a more general activity for a grade level, team, or department.

First, list each professional role that currently or could in the future co-teach. Next, have the specialists in those roles complete the middle column, as specifically as possible listing all the contributions they make in a general education setting. In the meantime, general educators should complete the final columns, jotting down questions they have about the expertise of their specialist colleagues.

After everyone has completed their part of the worksheet, specialists should share the information they noted, and general educators should raise their questions.

1. What did this exercise teach you about your current or potential co-teaching?

2. What are key misunderstandings about roles and responsibilities?

3. What strategies could assist you and your teaching partner to avoid miscommunication about your co-teaching practice?

Professional Role	Specific Co-Teaching Contributions	Possible Partner Questions

Questions to Clarify Practices Similar to Co-Teaching

The following questions could be applied to any practice at your school that is called co-teaching, but that doesn't meet the criteria established, whether the ones discussed in this chapter or others, including the supports provided by paraprofessionals. These questions are best used to help all staff members understand the essential elements of the practices they are implementing.

1. Using information from Chapter 1 as well as other chapters, what are the key characteristics of co-teaching that define it as a service delivery options for students with disabilities or other special needs?

2. In what ways is the practice you're discussing consistent with the defining characteristics of co-teaching as described in this manual?

3. In what ways is the practice you're discussing inconsistent with the defining characteristics of co-teaching as described in this manual?

4. How did the practice you're discussing come to be called co-teaching? Were there specific reasons? Was it inadvertent or deliberate?

5. Why does it make a difference whether a practice is given an accurate name?

6. What is an alternative name the practice you're discussing could be given? How could you encourage others to use this label for the practice?

Co-Teaching Schedule Variations

Use this chart to analyze current and possible co-teaching practices. In the first row, note the model currently in place and brainstorm its advantages and disadvantages. Then consider other options. For some or all of those listed, note the advantages and disadvantages of each. Is the current option satisfactory? If not, what other options should be further explored for the next school year?

Schedule Variation	Advantages	Disadvantages
Current practices:		
Alternatives:		
Full day		
Half-day		
2 classes/period		
Half-co-taught, half pullout services		
Every-other-day		
Other options		

Chapter 8
Frequently Asked Co-Teaching Questions

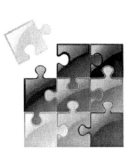

There are no extra pieces in the universe. Everyone is here because he or she has a place to fill, and every piece must fit itself into the big jigsaw puzzle.
~Deepak Chopra

Learner Objectives

1. Examine co-teaching questions involving teachers' professional relationships and apply strategies for responding to partnership dilemmas that may arise.

2. Identify co-teaching questions concerning program structure and other co-teaching practicalities, and assess a variety of options for overcoming logistics challenges.

3. Consider co-teaching questions relating to instruction, students' educational needs and parents' concerns, and special services delivery, and analyze suggestions for addressing issues in this domain.

One goal threaded throughout this book has been to provide answers for common questions about co-teaching, and I hope the pages you have already reviewed have addressed many of your concerns. However, in working with teachers, administrators, and other professionals across the U.S. and around the world, some questions and concerns span several of the areas covered in the preceding chapters, or they seem to need special emphasis. That is the purpose of this chapter. In the following sections you will find questions raised by educators in urban, suburban, and rural school districts and across many types of schools, some completely traditional and some highly innovative. Each question is accompanied by a response that is a combination of solutions others have found, my observations based on a long career of fostering effective co-teaching practices, and when available, what is known through research. Some of the topics may not apply to your situation at all, but others may reflect exactly the challenge that you face. Some of the questions are particularly applicable to professionals at elementary, middle, or high schools while others are pertinent across grade levels. Some concern co-teaching with a particular specialist (e.g., a special educator or ESL teacher), but others are applicable across professional partnerships. If you have not found information on a specific issue elsewhere in this manual, perhaps you will find what you are looking for here. However, keep in mind that each of these questions could have several answers, and you might find that you would respond differently. I might respond in a different way, too, or at least in more detail, if the number of pages that could be devoted to each question was limitless.

This chapter is organized into three parts. In the first part, concerns about the partnerships between teachers are considered, and in the second part questions about co-teaching program structure and logistics are presented. The final section includes items related to instruction; students and families; and the delivery of special education, ESL, and other special services.

Questions and Concerns about Teacher Partnerships

Many of the questions that arise concerning co-teaching relate to the working relationships teachers develop and the difficulties they encounter in sustaining partnerships (e.g., Ploessl, Rock, Schoenfeld, & Blanks, 2010; Sims, 2008). As you consider the questions in this section, what should be more striking than anything is the importance of strong collaboration skills as a foundation for co-teaching success.

♣ **My co-teacher and I don't have a lot of planning time, and that is not going to change. I could manage if I had the lesson plans in advance, but my co-teacher just doesn't give them to me. She says she usually doesn't write them up until right before instruction. I suspect this is because our principal doesn't review them — they just have to exist if requested. How should I handle this situation without causing a problem?**

Not having the information needed to prepare for teaching can be frustrating, but it also can become a legal issue. That is, the special educator is charged with ensuring that students with disabilities are receiving the instruction they need and the accommodations that will facilitate their learning. The ESL teacher is mandated to address the students' needs as outlined in their individual learning plans. Without having lesson plans, it becomes nearly impossible to deliver those services.

The first step in addressing this matter usually is a conversation. The specialist should note the problem and request a solution using words such as these: "I'm very concerned about our students with special needs, especially making sure they're receiving their required services. I have to have lesson plans in advance in order to do my part. What options could we try so that I could have at least a couple of days to prepare?"

Of course, two days is not always adequate preparation time, but the specialist has to be willing to compromise. It would be more effective to receive lesson plans a week or more in advance, as recommended in Chapter 6, but if that is not possible some lead time is better than none at all. Ultimately, if this dilemma is interfering with the delivery of special education or ESL services, it may become a matter needing input from an administrator.

I'm co-teaching in middle school and struggling to keep up with the curriculum. Sometimes during class my teaching partner suddenly asks me to teach something — no warning, no preparation. Then she uses my discomfort as proof that special educators shouldn't be in general education classrooms. What should I do?

To understand this situation, think about the general educator's reason for asking the specialist to teach extemporaneously. Even though it sounds like a form of resistance, it could be that the teacher is poorly prepared and often does the same thing, and so he hopes his partner can help cover the day's instruction. It also could be a matter of the general educator realizing the specialist has not led instruction in a while and really should not thinking through the discomfort this well-intentioned behavior causes. In other words, the thinking behind this awkward situation may be benign.

Whatever the motive for the general education teacher's actions, being proactive might help. For example, the specialist might mention during a planning session that she appreciates the general educator's awareness of the need for her to lead instruction, but that she is not yet comfortable enough with the content to lead without time to prepare. She could then suggest that either they could designate particular lessons coming up in which she might lead a specific activity or discussion, or she could suggest that they try a co-teaching approach that could help on this matter and utilize the specialist's expertise for specially designed instruction. Perhaps they could team, with the special educator interjecting examples and clarifying vocabulary for students. Perhaps they could team for a brief large-group lesson and then divide the students into stations with each teacher working with a group of students on an application or discussion of the day's material. This matter should be addressed sooner rather than later to avoid establishing patterns in the co-taught class that are difficult to change.

✦ **Through strong support and careful planning by my principal, my co-teacher and I have weekly shared planning time. However, she sometimes comes to it late, sometimes cancels, and occasionally just never shows up. Now what?**

When one co-teacher occasionally misses a planning session, it probably is the result of a particularly hectic day, a crisis, or a miscommunication — and should not be a source of concern. However, if shared planning time is allocated but often not used, it becomes a matter of accountability, and it also could become a threat to co-teaching program integrity. As you might suspect, the teacher who shows up on time probably will have to begin the conversation that addresses this matter (whether the general educator or the specialist). She might note that the scheduled planning time does not seem to be working out very well. The next step is to listen to the response of the other professional. Perhaps having planning time right after students have lunch is causing a problem. In a large high school, it might be the location for the planning — by the time the person who is late wraps up the preceding class, gathers materials, and walks to the planning location (being stopped repeatedly along the way by colleagues who wish to chat), being late is almost inevitable.

As for several other topics mentioned in this section, conversation is critical (e.g., Sileo, 2011). If the reason for the issue can be identified, then perhaps the planning time can be modified, the start time delayed by ten minutes (to allow for extra transit time), or the location changed. If the co-teachers are experienced, perhaps they could meet every other week instead of every week, with the alternate week used to address some of the matters interfering with planning. This problem also could be one where input from others is helpful. If other teachers also have shared planning time, they may have suggestions on how to ensure it is used wisely.

Finally, mention must be made of the focus for the planning. The teacher who comes late or misses the planning session may not perceive that the joint planning has enough value to make it a priority. If that is the case, the teachers probably should clarify their expectations, state their agenda, and renew their commitment to this critical aspect of co-teaching.

✦ **In many ways, co-teaching is more difficult than working with a student teacher. The specialist assigned to work with me causes many problems during class. She often makes comments or provides examples during instruction that are inaccurate, and she spends so much time helping students in the class — babying**

them — that they will never reach their potential. I'm at the point where I'd rather teach alone than with a partner. Should I suggest this as an option?

It may be tempting to abandon co-teaching in this difficult situation, but the repercussions could be serious. In particular, because co-teaching is being used as the mechanism through which students are receiving their mandated services, your assessment of the situation cannot be justification for halting those services. In fact, another way of delivering the services probably would have to be found, a nearly impossible expectation in many schools. At the same time, if the specialist is causing problems with instruction, the topic must be discussed. You might say something like this to your teaching partner: "When we both try to provide information to the students, I'm worried that it confuses them. You're very observant and know when they are getting confused during large-group instruction. Instead of trying to explain concepts another way, I'd really appreciate it if you would directly let me know that students seem confused. Then we could stop to see what questions students have or to use your skills to teach a strategy, add examples, or give them extra visuals to help their understanding." The goal is not to remove your partner from instruction; it is to first try to utilize her expertise.

The related topic of babying students likewise requires discussion. It is best to have conversations about expectations for specific students prior to the beginning of an instructional unit, being careful to provide mandated supports but at the same time to challenge students so that they grow. You could identify one or two examples of what you mean by babying, and you and your partner could try various approaches, gathering data to see if you could nudge students to a higher level. Part of the reason this disagreement occurs is because of the different perspectives professionals have about students and the instructional process, a topic addressed in Chapter 3.

I'm ready! I'd like to try as many new ideas as possible to enhance co-teaching, but my partner seems to be completely happy to keep things as they are, which is not really co-teaching at all, and doesn't want to try anything new. One of us delivers the instruction and the other provides support and remediation. What should I do?

When one half of the partnership is reluctant, co-teaching tends to stagnate. Addressing this issue requires your willingness to raise the topic and use effective communication skills to discuss options. Exactly what you say depends partly on whether you are the general educator or the specialist. However, a first step in knowing how to respond is trying to understand the other person's point of view.

If you are the general educator working with a reluctant specialist, consider that professional's perspective. Is the person uncomfortable with the content? Fearful of making a mistake and of what your reaction might be? Intimidated by your level of content knowledge and skill? Concerned that you consider the classroom yours and might be put off with another professional's input? You could try several conversation starters to allay these potentially problematic beliefs and enhance co-teaching. For example, you might say something like this: "I've been reading about co-teaching and ways it can look. Next week I'd like to try something new." Then offer your idea of a new approach to try or a new way to assign roles in the classroom. One specific recommendation is to gauge your suggestion on the apparent comfort level of the other educator. If you sense the reluctance is because of lack of content knowledge, you might propose dividing students during a review but not for initial instruction. If you sense the reluctance is because of overall stress about being in the general education setting, you might propose station teaching, an option that puts students into relatively small groups and permits each teacher to deliver the same instruction multiple times.

If you are a specialist working with a reluctant general educator, your analysis of the situation might be a bit different. Does the general educator perceive that you are judging the quality of his teaching? Believe that students with disabilities or those learning English should be in general education settings only if they can keep up with the already-established instructional content and activities? Sense that your presence interferes with the instructional flow and your input results in slowing down the pace of instruction and the ability to cover all the required content?

As advised for general educators, your response should take into account your understanding of the other person's point of view. Depending on your situation, you might raise the topic in this way: "I've been thinking about our co-teaching. I know others are expecting us to raise student achievement but also to meet our students' special needs. I'm not sure that what we're doing right now will lead to that result, but I have a couple of ideas we might try." As in the other scenario, it is important to suggest an idea that addresses the other professional's comfort level, perhaps starting with you taking notes on the Smartboard™ while the other person delivers a brief lecture, or proposing that you do the warm-up activity at the beginning of the class or the wrap-up activity at its conclusion. As these options succeed additional, more integrated options can be added.

Regardless of your role, you should try at least three times to raise the topic and explore ways to address it. If none of your efforts is successful, you might try to involve a colleague who could provide informal input (such as an instructional coach), or you could ask for a meeting of all co-teachers so that ideas can be shared — and perhaps implemented by the reluctant participant. Your last resort, and one that may have serious negative repercussions, is to ask your co-teacher to meet with you and an administrator. This strategy usually conveys that your discomfort has grown to an intolerable level and that you believe students are not getting the education to which they are entitled.

✣ **At my school, we were doing well as co-teachers, gradually using more of the approaches and seeing real growth for students. But now we have a new teacher evaluation system, and some general education teachers want to stop co-teaching because they are worried that having students with special needs in their classes and sharing instruction could lead to lower ratings. Eventually, that could affect their pay.**

The new generation of teacher evaluation systems, whatever their advantages and disadvantages, has caused a great deal of stress for teachers and other professionals. Without explicit discussion about the system and clarification about what it means for co-teachers, situations such as the one described in this question are common.

In addressing this area of uncertainty, several points should be made. First, and at the broadest level, the notion that teachers can decide that they do not want to teach students with disabilities or other special needs because of teacher evaluation is troubling. These students have a right to be educated, and most of them have a right to be in the general education setting. Teachers who think they should be able to choose their student groups are forgetting that they are public school teachers and that they are required by law to effectively teach whichever students walk through their doors, whether or not they have special needs. In addition, when such students' services are appropriately provided in the context of general education, co-teaching becomes a necessity. What the most successful co-teachers have found is that sharing instruction does not lead to lower teacher ratings — instead, the teachers' combined efforts lead to such improved student outcomes that other teachers often are jealous of what the co-teachers have accomplished.

To understand the teacher evaluation system and its use with co-teachers, professionals should request that administrators explain how the assessment instrument will be used and the procedure that will be followed in co-taught classes. In some cases, two observers will come to the co-taught class, simultaneously assessing the two teachers while they conduct a typical lesson. In others, the observer will focus on one teacher, even though both professionals are teaching. Occasionally, one observer will gather data on both teachers in a single lesson. One approach not recommended is to have one of the partners assume a passive role in the classroom while the other is observed. This intimates that co-teaching is not valued, that teacher evaluation is premised on a professional working alone. Frequently, administrators appropriately decide that a professional who co-teaches should be observed in that environment as well as in a solo-taught class.

If you are concerned about teacher evaluation systems, especially as they apply to special educators, you might download and share with your colleagues the position statement on this topic by the Council for Exceptional Children (2012); details on locating it are included in the reference list. Although it may not be a comforting thought, keep in mind that this topic is likely to be a focus for professional debate for the next several years.

Questions and Concerns about Co-Teaching Program Structure and Logistics

Because each school has a set of unique characteristics that affect the options for arranging co-teaching, shared planning time, and student assignment to classes, the number of issues that arise related to co-teaching program structure and logistics should sometimes seems limitless. These are some of the most common questions about setting up co-teaching programs in a way that makes them integral to the overall school schedule and feasible in terms of most effectively and efficiently utilizing personnel resources.

I am a specialist who co-teaches nearly fulltime. However, when a general education teacher in the school is absent I'm often told to cancel co-teaching to cover that teacher's class. Is this appropriate?

Professionals generally understand that if a flu epidemic is spreading across the community and substitute teachers cannot be found, any available professional may be called to help ensure that the educational process is not disrupted for students. However, such situations should be rare rather than common. If specialists are asked nearly every week to divert their attention from providing students' services to substitute teach, both legal and ethical issues should be raised. First, each time co-teaching does not occur, students are missing the services to which they are entitled based on their IEPs or ILPs. Especially for special educators, a pattern of failure to deliver services because of re-assigning them to other responsibilities could result in legal liability.

An ethical concern should be mentioned as well. What does this practice say about the value of the co-teaching partnership? Is it a message that the presence of the second professional in the classroom is so limited in impact that it is more important to have that person cover another class? Is it a strategy of convenience — that is, is it easier to re-assign the specialist than to distribute the students to other classes, as should occur? Whatever the thinking behind this decision, it is a topic that should be raised with a sympathetic administrator and directly discussed. Untenured and early career professionals may not feel they can risk broaching this topic, and so it may fall to experienced, tenured professionals to do this.

❖ **At our elementary school, we begin the year with everything set up and all students receiving their services. But we have a lot of transience, and so students move in and get placed in classes without co-teaching. Also, we usually identify a number of students during the year, and they're often in classes without co-teaching. How do we make sure they get their services?**

What is described in this question is perhaps the most common scheduling dilemma of elementary schools. No ideal answer exists, but strategies such as these can help to alleviate this problem:

♦ If a student is identified as having a disability or needing ESL services during the first couple of weeks of the school year, in some situations it might be possible to re-assign the student to the class in which co-teaching is already occurring.

♦ Specialists in schools where this problem occurs every year should design their schedules with dilemma in mind, keeping several slots of time open to accommodate the students who move into the district and those identified during the course of the school year. This time can be used for assessment, observation, and short-term support until needed for co-teaching.

♦ Some students' services may have to be in a pullout environment for the remainder of the school year in which they are identified or enroll. This time would come from one of the slots noted above. Alternatively, specialists might blend some of their services. If two special educators share responsibilities in a school, one may provide services to the other's newly identified student. If one ESL teacher is teaching in a separate setting, a student from the other ESL teacher's caseload might need to access those services. Notice that this solution requires specialists to collaborate in designing their services. Also, although the next logical step would be for ESL teachers and special educators to cover for each other, in most instances policies prohibit this blending of special services, even if it seems like it could be effective.

❖ **We're in the third year of our co-teaching program. Our principal has based co-teaching on volunteers, and next year none of the general education teachers want to participate. What happens if no one volunteers?**

Who co-teaches is a matter for administrative attention rather than a teacher responsibility. If co-teaching is the needed service for students, then it has to be offered. It is not really a matter of whether teachers are volunteering. Even though that sounds harsh, basing services on teachers' preferences cannot be justified legally or ethically.

The underlying question that might need to be addressed is why so much reluctance is being encountered. Are too many students with special needs being assigned to a single classroom? Are teachers reluctant because they fear not being able to communicate with their students primarily speak languages other than English? Is the support offered to the students and teachers appropriate? If the professionals work to understand the factors leading to this difficult situation, then the likelihood of addressing them and finding workable solutions rises dramatically.

✦ **No matter what we do, the co-taught class gets behind other sections of the same course. We don't want to skip anything, but we constantly worry that when it's time for testing, the students in the co-taught class are at a disadvantage because they have not learned everything the other students have mastered.**

When co-taught classes are falling behind solo-taught classes, alarm bells definitely should be going off in teachers' and administrators' heads. Co-teaching is not intended to slow instruction to the point that critical instruction does not happen, and students in co-taught classes must be as prepared for high-stakes testing as other students. Two educators in the classroom has as its purpose ensuring that the intensity of instruction can increase, which should permit the pacing to stay approximately the same as in other classes.

Analysis of this problem should consider several possibilities. First, class composition should be reviewed. Has the class group been assigned in accordance with the guidelines mentioned in Chapter 6? That is, is there a cluster of students with special needs surrounded by a heterogeneous mix of classmates? If not, the first step to improve pacing is to adjust the class composition. Second, what co-teaching approaches are being used? Are they the most efficient and effective? As mentioned in Chapter 4, one problem could be that if much of the instruction is whole-group with both teachers contributing, their talk time may actually be interfering with the pace of instruction. In addition, whole-group instruction may be detracting from the pace of student learning that would be possible in arrangements emphasizing groups, such as station teaching or parallel teaching.

A third factor that may affect pacing concerns classroom procedures. How long does it take students to move from group to group? If your answer is more than 30-45 seconds, then valuable instructional time is being unnecessarily wasted. In fact, experienced co-teachers sometimes set a high expectation that students will move from one activity to another in under 30 seconds. Students should be taught the expectation and procedure for moving between activities in their co-taught class, and they should be rewarded for appropriately doing so. As an interim strategy to address this dilemma, teachers should (as possible) move among the class groups rather than losing time by having students move.

♦ I'm assigned to co-teach in seven classrooms each day. I'm so busy running from class to class that I'm never really focused on any single co-teaching lesson. Is it reasonable to expect me to co-teach in this number of classes?

When staffing and the way students are assigned to classes create this dilemma, it is time to step back to re-assess the entire program structure. First, this may have occurred because of students being identified or moving in during the course of the school year, and it might be best to have some students receive services in a separate setting for the remainder of the year. Second, this could have resulted because of a decision related to the initial assignment of students to classes. That is, a principal may have decided that in order to be "fair," students should be distributed across all classrooms. Third, this could have occurred when scheduling was managed through computer software without taking into account the need for co-taught sections.

This problem can be avoided by addressing its source. In the meantime, here are some other thoughts on this topic: Usually, special educators and ESL teachers who are co-teaching can do so in one or two classes or sections their first year, eventually increasing the number to three or four sections as programs evolve and responsibilities change. Occasionally, a specialist even manages a fifth assignment. However, when the number of classes assigned for co-teaching is as high as seven, a more realistic way of looking at the services is to decide which ones are really another form of service and deliver it accordingly. That is, one of the classes may actually need only consultative support, and this should be specified and offered. Another class may need periodic support and not a daily partnership. Specialists in this situation should actively discuss this topic with their administrators, looking forward to the next semester or school year to make decisions about how to re-structure the co-teaching program to raise the feasibility — and thus the quality — of the specialized services delivered through it.

♦ As a special educator in an inclusive school, I feel like I can't do it all. I'm supposed to co-teach in several classes, pull students for remedial instruction, keep up with all the paperwork, attend meetings (that seem to get scheduled when I'm supposed to be co-teaching), communicate with parents, and do anything else that comes along. Do others feel this way?

Yes, they do. Co-teaching requires adjustments on the part of all educators, and for special educators, those adjustments can be significant. Feeling inundated can be particularly stressful when programs move quickly from traditional formats to innovative ones. The sense of being overwhelmed may be mostly perception, but it also could indicate problems in the program structure. For example, is the special educator trying to co-teach across content areas in a high school and not able to keep up with the curriculum? Is an elementary special educator trying to keep traditional pullout services for most students while at the same time also trying to co-teach?

Addressing the problem requires finding its source and designing ways to address the core problems. A strategy as simple as having special education staff members meet to discuss their experiences may help, as may having teachers visit successful co-teaching programs in nearby schools. Another possibility is doing a job analysis for the special educator to identify whether any services are being duplicated, whether some students might be receiving too much service (thereby causing problems in terms of workload for the special educator), or whether services could be re-arranged in order to streamline them.

♣ **I teach in the related arts (that is, art, music, physical education, drama, media/technology). I work with nearly every student in the school who has an IEP or who is an English language learner. However, I have no support at all, neither a co-teacher nor a paraprofessional. Shouldn't I be entitled to some type of assistance just like all the other teachers?**

Related arts classes as well as electives (for example, psychology, web design) or non-core academic classes (for example, Spanish I) seem to be short-changed when co-teaching programs are designed. A review of support needs in such classes should occur right along with the analysis completed for core academic courses. If all students must take and pass a keyboarding class, a decision to provide co-teaching in that class may be justified. However, professionals need to have direct conversations about priorities and resources. While it would be wonderful to have co-teaching available in every middle and high school course, this is not warranted, nor is it usually feasible. In some schools paraprofessionals are assigned to such classes, at least on a part-time basis, so some assistance can be available even if daily fulltime support cannot be offered. A message that does not seem kind but that is nonetheless true is that students with special needs are not entitled to support in every class taken, and for electives and non-core academic courses, no option for adding such support may exist.

Whether you work in an elementary, middle, or high school, do be sure that all professionals, including those in the related arts and other courses, are part of the conversations about how to design effective services for students who are ELLs and those with disabilities. By considering all participants' perspectives during program design and making sure the concerns of these valuable staff members are on the table along with those of the other educators, options for addressing them (even if they cannot be completely resolved) are more likely.

Questions and Concerns related to Students, Parents, and the Delivery of Instruction and Specialized Services

The trend to educate students with special needs in general education settings in no way reduces the obligation of professionals to be sure students receive high quality instruction as well as their special services, whether those relate to special education, ESL programs, or both. A companion obligation is to maintain clear communication with parents concerning the general instructional program, special services, and student matters. The following questions are frequently asked by today's co-teachers.

Do the Common Core State Standards (CCSS) support co-teaching?

As you know, the CCSS (possibly given an alternative name as part of implementation in your state) are intended to increase rigor and ensure that today's students have the knowledge and skills necessary for success in the 21st-century global community, that students are college and career ready. The CCSS have distilled the many standards and priorities that characterized education during the latter part of the 20th century, focusing on relevance and a problem-based approach to current and future learning. Much information now is available about the CCSS. You can begin your investigation of the rationale for and understanding of this initiative at the CCSS Initiative website (2012), included in the reference list for this chapter.

The CCSS do not provide specific curriculum, nor do they prescribe how the standards should be addressed in schools, and thus they in no way offer guidance on co-teaching. However, co-teachers are finding that their partnerships are essential in helping students to master the standards. First, think about the level of academic vocabulary and problem solving skills required. Both students with disabilities and ELLs are likely to struggle in these areas, and two teachers available to work with students, scaffolding their learning, are more likely to effectively address the standards than a general education teacher or specialist working alone. In addition, the CCSS stresses the integration of literature in social studies and science; this challenging expectation is far more easily managed in a co-taught class than a solo-taught class. If you map the expectations of the CCSS onto the options that are created through co-teaching, you will find that, although co-teaching is not part of the CCSS, it definitely can assist teachers in moving all their students to new levels of learning.

🧩 **The students in the co-taught classroom are functioning several grade levels below other students. How is it possible to address these students' goals in the context of a fast-paced general education classroom where emphasis is on learning the grade level curriculum?**

This question reflects the collision between traditional thinking about special and ESL education and emerging contemporary practices. For students with disabilities, one part of this issue raises questions about how IEPs are being written. For nearly all students with disabilities, the aim now is to base instruction in the grade level curriculum, even if students' skills are assessed at a lower level. For example, if the sixth grade curriculum has a standard about students being able to listen critically and offer reasoned opinions, backed by evidence, an IEP oral language goal should be written within this grade level expectation. That is, the student might carry out the grade level proficiency but do so having listened to a simpler passage. In today's schools, IEP goals should not exist in a vacuum; they must relate to grade level standards.

Similar comments could be made concerning students who are English language learners. That is, for most students, the goal is to simultaneously guarantee access to the same curriculum as typical classmates while providing scaffolding and language instruction embedded within that curriculum. Thus, some students will address grade level standards using materials written at a different level or through sheltered English instruction incorporated into the general education setting.

Another dimension to this question concerns integrating necessary remediation for some students. For young students where the concern is reading and language arts skills, these needs should be addressed as part of the overall language arts program (e.g., Whittaker, 2012). That is, elementary programs should include a segment of time each day when students are grouped based on their assessed needs; during this time the most struggling readers would be together to receive intensive instruction.

Yet another aspect of this question may relate to the level of student needs and the flexibility for meeting them. Professionals could decide that for a few students, an intensive instructional arrangement in a separate setting is necessary (e.g., Calderon, Slavin, & Sanchez, 2011). If this is the case, they should not think that this is not allowed, but they should gather detailed data to determine whether using this more restrictive instructional environment produces the intended results. If it does, it can be continued, but if it does not then it cannot be justified.

Delivering special education and ESL services in today's schools has become a complicated business. Clearly, students must receive their specialized instruction and related services. At the same time, services must be offered in the least restrictive environment for students with disabilities and in the setting that will most foster growth for ELLs; the presumption in most cases is that the general education classroom is strongly preferred. Layered on these expectations are the mandates in current legislation that students have access to the general curriculum as it is taught by teachers highly qualified in the content areas. The task for professionals is to keep a healthy tension among all of these factors so that students can reach their potential.

How should co-teaching be indicated on a student's IEP?

Questions about co-teaching and IEPs usually arise when no state or local policy exists regarding this matter. If you are wondering about this topic, your first strategy should be to check with a special education administrator to see if guidelines for noting co-teaching are in place. In some states and districts, co-teaching is listed separately as a means through which a student will receive special education services. In others, co-teaching is written in as the instructional procedure with the setting listed as general education. In yet others, co-teaching is considered being educated in general education with direct service provided there. In a few locales, co-teaching is not noted on IEPs at all, partly because of fear that when implementation is uneven across the schools in a district, specifying co-teaching on the IEP may lead to problems if the student transfers to a school not implementing it.

Because so many policies exist regarding indicating co-teaching on IEPs, no single answer can be given. If you are unable to obtain a definitive answer locally, you should at least be consistent in how you (and your colleagues who also are writing IEPs) specify that co-teaching is being provided.

What does co-teaching look like for students with significant intellectual disabilities? Should they be part of this model for providing special education services?

This is another question that has no single answer, and it can only be discussed based on local policies and beliefs as well as individual student needs. Experience suggests that students with significant disabilities can benefit greatly when they are part of a co-teaching program (e.g., Ryndak, Ward, Alper, Montgomery, & Storch, 2010). This practice can help to meet the IDEA requirement that they receive their education in the least restrictive environment. In a few communities, these students may spend most of their school day in a classroom supported through co-teaching and, possibly, paraprofessional support. This is most likely to occur at the elementary level. In most regions of the country, though, co-teaching for students with significant intellectual disabilities occurs on a part-time basis, often dependent on specific student needs and staffing. One common pattern is for these students to join a class already being co-taught by a teacher for students with mild or moderate disabilities. By using this approach, the teacher in the separate class can remain there while the students who participate in general education continue to receive special education support. An alternative is for a paraprofessional to accompany these students, offering support in the general education setting. Again, this strategy for co-teaching is most often seen at the elementary level. In secondary settings, student participation often is limited to related arts and elective classes such as art and music. As noted earlier, the support for such situations is most likely to be a paraprofessional rather than a co-teacher.

It should be mentioned that this question has many layers of implications. The high-stakes testing and accountability climate in today's schools has resulted, in some communities, in students with significant intellectual disabilities largely being excluded from participation in core general education content, usually justified on the fact that these students take an alternate assessment and cannot be allowed to "interfere" with the instruction that must be delivered to other students. In other schools, the notion of students with significant intellectual disabilities participating in co-teaching has not even been considered. If this is a topic of discussion in your school, it may be one that is appropriate for a careful and reflective dialogue about inclusive belief systems and the service delivery options used in inclusive schools.

🧩 **Our co-teaching group has been discussing who should communicate with parents. If a specialist calls or e-mails the parent of a student who does not have special needs, will it raise parents' concerns? If the general education teacher communicates, does it imply the student is not receiving services? If co-teaching is partnership, should we both participate in all student conferences — which doesn't seem feasible?**

Co-teachers are wise to directly discuss parent communication so that problems such as those mentioned can be avoided. As is true of so many aspects of co-teaching, decisions about communication should represent the balance between what would be ideal and the reality of busy professionals.

The first strategy for ensuring clear parent communication is to decide whether information about the two-teacher class should be shared with parents at the beginning of the school year. If you are in a school district in which co-teaching occurs in any single classroom for half or more of the day, this step definitely is needed. If co-teaching occurs for a relatively short period of time in elementary or only in a few classes in a middle or high school setting, this approach may raise more issues than it prevents. In those situations, educators may decide that the general educator (keeping the specialist informed, of course) may contact any parent of a student in the class while the specialist contacts parents of students on their caseloads as needed, but the parents of other students only with prior discussion with the general educator.

Parent conferences are another matter to discuss (e.g., Guo, 2010). In most schools, it is not possible for specialists to attend every parent conference for the students in the co-taught classes. Instead, professionals usually focus first on having both teachers at the conferences of the students eligible for special services. They then decide if it would be helpful to arrange for both of them to participate in any other conferences and next prioritize scheduling those. Note that teachers should consider carefully whether two professionals conducting a parent conference might be intimidating to some parents (for example, those unfamiliar with the U.S. school system; those who may have had many negative experiences with interactions with school professionals).

I was surprised when several parents of students with disabilities told me they did not want their children in co-taught classes; they want instruction in the separate setting to be continued. Does this mean that we shouldn't co-teach?

A decision about the education environment most appropriate for a student with a disability is made by the team that writes the IEP, not by the teachers, other professionals alone, or individual parents. Placement must be based on the assessed needs of the student, the type of instruction needed, the mandate of the least restrictive environment, and the supplementary aids and services that can be provided to support the student in a general education setting.

If a parent is worried about a co-taught class, you should ask what the concern is. Some parents like the idea of a small, highly structured class and value the protection of their children over the rising achievement expectations (and related pressure and stress). Parents of students in high school — students who may for most of their education have been in separate settings for core academic instruction — may truly question whether their children can be successful and accepted in general education. For the first group of parents, it might be possible to suggest an IEP be implemented for a defined period of time (such as one grading period) and then reviewed. For the latter group of parents, the reluctance is understandable and it may not be appropriate to make a dramatic shift in services during a student's final year or two of school.

Professionals' responsibility to all parents of students with disabilities is to listen carefully to their concerns, ask questions to obtain a fuller understanding, and then try to work with parents to find a solution. Co-teaching often is a way to provide special education services in the least restrictive environment, but it is not the only option that should exist (and it cannot be the only service available to students, ignoring their specific needs). Each student's situation must be considered individually by the IEP team and decisions reached based on the student's assessed needs and goals written and in partnership with parents (Lalvani, 2012).

The parents of one of the students in our class, a student who is an average learner, have complained to our principal that they do not want their child in co-teaching and will go to the school board if he is not moved to another class. Is a parent allowed to make this type of demand?

Most parents of typical learners are either unaware of the co-teaching program in their children's school, or they are strongly supportive of the benefits of co-teaching their children derive. When parents express concerns, professionals first should try to understand the basis for them. Just as with parents of students with disabilities, listening is the beginning point. Some parents may have a vague concern that the students with special needs will somehow cause the instruction to be watered down or standards to be lowered. This concern should be laid to rest. Other parents may object to their children being educated with the students they refer to as "those kids." What they may not realize is that their children have always been in classes with students with disabilities or other special needs; co-teaching programs and bringing special services into the general education setting usually is the only change occurring, not the membership of the class.

Administrators and teachers should be respectful of parent perspectives and attempt to address concerns, but acquiescing to parents' requests to place their children in particular classrooms and not in others can lead to a sort of contagion of rejection. The direct answer to this question is that public schools are just that — public schools — and parents do not have the option of deciding which children should be their children's classmates. This is a matter for principals to address; they often ask parents to describe their children's characteristics and then gently inform them that the final decision about class assignment is one that school professionals, not parents, make. One principal learned this lesson the hard way: In the first year of co-teaching he invited parents to volunteer their children for co-taught classes, and no one volunteered. He was placed in the position of making decisions that were perceived by parents as broken promises. The next year (and every year since then), he adopted a policy of creating class groups based on input from teachers and parents, but with his final decision. What could have remained a significant source of conflict is now seldom mentioned.

One final comment on this topic should be made. Occasionally, parents will voice a legitimate concern about their child's placement. For example, if a student with a disability has been physically aggressive with their child or if their child has been repeatedly asked to assist a child learning English or who has disability, their concerns should be addressed. Overall, though, this problem occurs only occasionally and usually can be solved with clear policies and respectful communication.

For Further Thought

1. Many of the professional partnership challenges addressed in this chapter could be prevented or quickly resolved through effective communication and emphasis on collaboration. Why do you think it is still difficult in many schools for professionals to speak with each other directly about issues related to their partnership? Do you think this varies by school level — elementary, middle, or high? Years of experience of the professionals co-teaching? On what experiences or readings are your responses based? What ideas do you have for reducing partnership issues in co-teaching?

2. As you review the topics in the section on program structure and logistics, consider how each (or a variation of each) pertains to your school. How are you addressing these topics? Why is administrative support so essential in addressing nearly every issue that was raised?

3. What steps would you suggest taking in a school just introducing co-teaching as a means of avoiding concerns raised by both parents of students with special needs and parents of typical learners? Which strategies might work at the elementary, middle, or high school level? Across all school levels?

Taking Action

1. With the issues raised in this chapter and others that may be concerns specific to your school as a starting point, create a brief survey to distribute to staff members. Use the information you gather to make recommendations about refining your co-teaching program and further educating those who are not direct participants about its structure and outcomes.

2. With a committee or task force, discuss issues that have arisen or may arise regarding co-teaching services. Then identify ways to directly address them. For those anticipated, identify and implement proactive strategies for sharing information that could prevent them from ever becoming a concern. Decide what data could help you monitor whether those issues are being resolved satisfactorily.

3. If your school is new to co-teaching or experiencing serious challenges to effective implementation, see if it would be possible for several professionals

to visit a school that has addressed similar matters. It is suggested that a set of goals be identified for this visit and questions be prepared to ask teachers and administrators at the school. After the visit, professionals should meet to ensure that the information they obtained as part of the visit is applied to the situation at their school, with a detailed action plan generated and implemented.

References

Calderon, M., Slavin, R., & Sanchez, M. (2011). Effective instruction for English learners. *Future of Children, 21*(1), 103-127.

Council for Exceptional Children. (2012). *Position on special education teacher evaluation.* Arlington, VA: Author. Retrieved from http://cec.sped.org/~/media/Files/Policy/CEC%20Professional%20Policies%20and%20Positions/Position_on_Special_Education_Teacher_Evaluation_Background.pdf.

Council of Chief State School Officers and National Governors Association. (2012). *Common core state standards initiative: Preparing America's students for college and career.* Retrieved from http://www.corestandards.org/.

Guo, Y. (2010). Meetings without dialogue: A study of ESL parent-teacher interactions at secondary school parents' nights. *School Community Journal, 20*(1), 121-140.

Lalvani, P. (2012). Parents' participation in special education in the context of implicit educational ideologies and socioeconomic status. *Education and Training in Autism and Developmental Disabilities, 47,* 474-486.

Ploessl, D., Rock, M., Schoenfeld, N., & Blanks, B. (2010). On the same page: Practical techniques to enhance co-teaching interactions. *Intervention in School and Clinic, 45,* 158-168.

Ryndak, D., Ward, T., Alper, S., Montgomery, J., & Storch, J. F. (2010). Long-term outcomes of services for two persons with significant disabilities with differing educational experiences: A qualitative consideration of the impact of educational experiences. *Education and Training in Autism and Developmental Disabilities, 45,* 323-338.

Sileo, J. M. (2011). Co-teaching: Getting to know your partner. *Teaching Exceptional Children, 43*(5), 32-38.

Sims, E. (2008). Sharing command of the co-teaching ship: How to play nicely with others. *English Journal, 97*(5), 58-63.

Whittaker, C. R. (2012). Integrating literature circles into a cotaught inclusive classroom. *Intervention in School and Clinic, 47,* 214-223.

Chapter 8 Appendix

The appendix for this chapter includes two items that are designed to summarize the materials address throughout Co-Teach! and to prompt you to apply what you have learned to your own practices. The first item is a set of questions intended to help co-teachers reflect on and extend their co-teaching. The second is a set of scenarios that have occurred in schools implementing co-teaching. They could be used for role playing or group discussion.

THE BIG TEN: ANALYSIS OF CO-TEACHING PRACTICE

The following ten areas summarize many topics addressed in *Co-Teach!* and have critical importance for the effective implementation of co-teaching. Other areas also are important — for example, many exist in the administrative domain, but this set can foster discussion of whether co-teaching will lead to effective student outcomes. Questions related to each area are included to facilitate your discussion.

1. **The co-teaching partnership**

   ♦ What are indicators of parity both in and outside the classroom?

   ♦ How do we understand our distinct roles in the classroom? How do we communicate to parents, students, and others our distinct roles?

   ♦ How mature is our ongoing communication?

2. **Six co-teaching approaches**

   ♦ What proportion of co-teaching time is spent in each approach?

   ♦ How are decisions made about which approach to use?

   ♦ How have the approaches been tailored to meet the needs of the students and the curriculum being taught and learned?

3. **Instruction — general and specially designed**

   ♦ To what extent are the instructional practices based on a research? If asked, could we summarize the research that contributes to the practice being considered effective?

   ♦ How are the specially designed instructional needs of students with disabilities directly addressed in the classroom? How are these interventions documented?

4. **Data collection, interpretation, and use**

   ♦ What are examples of instructional data regularly gathered in the co-taught classroom? How are they recorded?

   ♦ How are instructional data used to plan instruction?

   ♦ How are data related to students' IEPs gathered (e.g., academic, behavior with disabilities)?   How are they recorded?

5. **Classroom environment**

   ♦ How has the classroom been adjusted (e.g., furniture, available or white boards, teacher work areas) to accommodate the needs of co-teachers.

   ♦ How have we directly created a supportive social and instructional environment for the diverse students in our co-taught class?

6. **Classroom management**

- ♦ What routines have we put in place so our classroom operates efficiently and effectively (e.g., moving from group to group; dealing with materials)?
- ♦ How do we make decisions regarding grouping of students in our co-taught class? How often are those decisions reviewed? To what extent are several grouping strategies used?
- ♦ How do we complete instructional chores, from set-up/clean-up to grading?

7. **Behavior management**

- ♦ To what extent do students respond equally to teachers on behavior matters?
- ♦ Who is responsible for addressing behavior issues in the classroom (e.g., giving rewards or negative consequences; leaving with a student who is disruptive)?
- ♦ How often is the special educator pulled from the co-teaching setting to respond to student behaviors in other classrooms or settings?

8. **Administrative support**

- ♦ How knowledgeable is our principal about co-teaching?
- ♦ How has our administrator addressed scheduling of planning time?
- ♦ How has our administrator addressed the appropriate scheduling of students with disabilities into general education classes, including those that are co-taught?

9. **Quality of planning**

- ♦ What schedule and process do we have in place for planning?
- ♦ If asked for documentation of our planning, including the implementation of SDI for students with disabilities, what could we provide?
- ♦ What role does technology play in our planning (e.g., Wiki, Edmodo)?

10. **Use of technology**

- ♦ How is technology used to gather, interpret, and use data in the co-taught class?
- ♦ How have we used co-teaching as a means of leveraging the effective use of instructional technology?
- ♦ What instructional and assistive technology are we using for students with disabilities and other special needs usually not available in a solo-taught class?

What Would You Do If...

Hopefully you will never encounter any of the scenarios described below. But they are all based on real events, and your colleagues at other schools and in other districts were faced with the problem of responding to them. Using everything you have learned in reading this manual, employ these situations as the basis for a role playing activity during staff development, or use them to discuss "what ifs" about your own co-teaching program. If you have been faced with a situation that you think could easily have been included here, focus discussion on that dilemma, too. Your goal should be to practice engaging in awkward discussions and reaching decisions about changes that could improve student outcomes while preserving professionals' working relationships.

Just Too Busy to Show Up

In an elementary school, many students' services are provided through co-teaching. Data suggest that students are learning more, and parents have voiced their satisfaction with the program. However, a problem is emerging as the school year progresses: One specialist has been missing a few minutes or a day here or there of her co-teaching. She explains that she has responsibilities for assessing students and must get that work completed in a timely manner, which necessitates skipping co-teaching. She also notes that she has reports to write and that when parents come to enroll their children, she may be needed for translating. She comments that she has to deal with many small crises as well, such as calming down a student whose behavior has become disruptive. The school's principal received a complaint from a usually supportive general educator about her partner's absence.

To role play or discuss:

Have one person be the missing co-teacher and the other be the general educator. Role play a meeting, scheduled for after school, to discuss what is occurring and what to do about it. Those observing should take notes and be ready to analyze the conversation. If you like, a third person could take on the role of the principal.

This is War!

A general educator explained his view of the classroom in this way: What goes on in the classroom is like a battlefield. Whether or not I'm victorious in getting students to learn depends on careful planning, watching all the players, being strategic, and taking necessary actions when surprises occur. And just like in a war, there can only be one general. I'm in charge, and anyone else in this classroom takes direction from me. That's just the way it is.

To role play or discuss:

Role play a meeting of co-teachers, with several pairs of participants. Have those involved discuss the teacher's comments and frame responses to them. One topic to introduce is that of alternative metaphors for co-teaching. How else could co-teaching be characterized, preferably in a way that is more conducive to classroom collaboration?

But We DO Collaborate…

In a high school English class, the partnership is awkward, to say the least. Privately, the general educator notes that two teachers in one class is not a good idea, that it interferes with the flow of instruction. At the same time, the specialist privately comments that with strong teachers who are opinionated, it's just not worth causing upset and so the best approach is one of "go along, get along." During a recently scheduled observation of the co-taught class, the principal discovered that the students needing special services, along with a few others with learning and behavior problems, had been pulled from class by the specialist to a conference room. There, they were being taught by the specialist, who spent considerable time addressing behavior. In the general education class, the English teacher was leading significantly different instruction, and she commented that she gets much more accomplished with the students who really want to learn when this arrangement is used. Upon investigation, the principal found that "this arrangement" was implemented 11 times over the past four weeks.

To role play or discuss:

Have one participant be a non-supervisory leader, such as a counselor, instructional coach, or psychologist. That person should facilitate a conversation between the two teachers about the purposes of co-teaching and their obligations related to instruction and specialized instruction. Alternatively, discuss how an administrator should handle this type of situation.

Notes

Notes

Notes

Notes